COVENANT

Leader Guide

Episodes 1–24

Abingdon Press™

Nashville

COVENANT BIBLE STUDY
LEADER GUIDE

ISBN 978-1-4267-7223-8

Magrey deVega, Leadership Editor for Covenant Bible Study

Scripture quotations are from the Common English Bible. Copyright © 2011 by the Common English Bible. All rights reserved. Used by permission. www.CommonEnglishBible.com.

Printed in China

14 15 16 17 18 19 20 21 22 23—10 9 8 7 6 5 4 3 2 1

Covenant Bible Study resources include:

Creating the Covenant: Participant Guide, ISBN 978-1-4267-7216-0
Living the Covenant: Participant Guide, ISBN 978-1-4267-7217-7
Trusting the Covenant: Participant Guide, ISBN 978-1-4267-7218-4
Covenant Bible Study App: Participant Guides for iOS and Android, ISBN 978-1-4267-7219-1

Covenant Bible Study: Covenant Meditations, ISBN 978-1-4267-7220-7
Covenant Bible Study: Covenant Meditations ePub, ISBN 978-1-4267-7221-4
Covenant Bible Study App: Covenant Meditations for iOS and Android, ISBN 978-1-4267-7222-1

Covenant Bible Study: Leader Guide, ISBN 978-1-4267-7223-8
Covenant Bible Study: Leader Guide eBook for eReaders, ISBN 978-1-4267-7225-2
Covenant Bible Study App: Leader Guide for iOS and Android, ISBN 978-1-4267-7224-5

Covenant Bible Study: DVD Video (set of three), ISBN 978-1-4267-8678-5
Covenant Bible Study: MP4 Video Episodes (download individually from CovenantBibleStudy.com)

CEB Study Bible, hardcover ISBN 978-1-6092-6028-6, decotone ISBN 978-1-6092-6040-8

To order resources or to obtain additional information for participants, Covenant groups, and leaders, go to www.CovenantBibleStudy.com or to www.cokesbury.com. All print resources are available exclusively from these online sites, from Cokesbury reps, or by calling Cokesbury (800-672-1789). The Covenant Bible Study digital app is available from iTunes and Google Play.

Contents

Basic Needs of a Covenant Group   14

Participant Guide 1: Creating the Covenant

Episode	Theme	Title	Page
1	Relationships	Creating the Covenant	19
2	Who Are We?	Torah: Genesis	27
3	Freedom and Instruction	Exodus, Leviticus, Numbers	31
4	God's Kingdom	Gospels: Matthew and Mark	35
5	Grace	Letters: Romans and Galatians	39
6	Witness	Hebrews	43
7	Logic of the Cross	1 and 2 Corinthians	47
8	Covenant Renewal	Deuteronomy, Joshua, Judges, 1 Samuel	51

Participant Guide 2: Living the Covenant

Episode	Theme	Title	Page
9	Faithful Love	Ruth, Esther, Song of Songs	55
10	The Spirit-Led Community	Luke and Acts	59
11	Leadership	2 Samuel, 1 and 2 Kings	63
12	God's Household	1 and 2 Thessalonians, 1 and 2 Timothy, Titus	67
13	Discernment	Wisdom: Proverbs and Ecclesiastes	71
14	Reconciled	Philemon, Philippians, Colossians, Ephesians	75
15	Act Like a Christian	James, Jude, 1 and 2 Peter	79
16	Doing the Right Thing	Prophets: Isaiah 1–39 and the Book of the Twelve	83

Participant Guide 3: Trusting the Covenant

Episode	Theme	Title	Page
17	Life Together	John; 1, 2, and 3 John	87
18	Praise and Lament	Psalms	91
19	Tragedy	Job	95
20	Crisis and Starting Over	Jeremiah, Lamentations, Ezekiel	99
21	Exile and Renewal	Isaiah 40–66	103
22	Restoration	1 and 2 Chronicles, Ezra, Nehemiah	107
23	Hope	Apocalyptic: Daniel	111
24	New Creation	Revelation	115

COVENANT
Leader Guide

COVENANT GROUP PARTICIPANTS AND LEADER

Name	Phone	E-mail

Covenant Group Meeting Location _____

Covenant Group Meeting Day and Time _____

CovenantBibleStudy.com username _____ password _____

Bible Readings at a Glance

Sign up your group at CovenantBibleStudy.com to send participants their daily readings by e-mail, and more.

Episode 2

Day 1	Genesis 1–3	Creation and the human role within it	❑
Day 2	Genesis 6:5–9:17; 11:1-9	End of the old world— beginning of the new world	❑
Day 3	Genesis 12; 15; 17; 22	Abraham and nationhood	❑
Day 4	Genesis 27–28; 32–33	Jacob and the biblical family	❑
Day 5	Genesis 37; 41; 43; 45; 50	Joseph and his brothers in Egypt	❑
Day 6	Covenant Meditation on Genesis 1:26-31	Who are we?	❑
Day 7	Group Meeting Experience with Genesis 9:7-17	The Bible's first covenant	❑

Episode 3

Day 1	Exodus 1–4	Oppression, survival, and the charge of a leader	❑
Day 2	Exodus 13:17–15:21	Crossing boundaries for freedom	❑
Day 3	Exodus 20–24	Sinai covenant	❑
Day 4	Leviticus 19–22	Holiness Code	❑
Day 5	Numbers 11–14	In the wilderness	❑
Day 6	Covenant Meditation on Leviticus 19:1-2	You must be holy because God is holy.	❑
Day 7	Group Meeting Experience with Exodus 20:1-17	Ten Commandments	❑

Episode 4

Day 1	Mark 1–4	God's kingdom is near.	❏
Day 2	Mark 12–14	God's kingdom is not here yet.	❏
Day 3	Matthew 4–7	New instruction for a new kingdom	❏
Day 4	Matthew 11–13	New way of life	❏
Day 5	Matthew 18–22	Jesus is the new Teacher.	❏
Day 6	Covenant Meditation on Mark 10:13-16	God's kingdom belongs to people like these.	❏
Day 7	Group Meeting Experience with Matthew 9:18-33	Jesus as deliverer	❏

Episode 5

Day 1	Romans 1–3	God's solution for the human condition	❏
Day 2	Galatians 1:1–3:5; 5:2-12	The sufficiency of Christ's sacrifice for salvation	❏
Day 3	Galatians 3:6–4:7; Romans 4	Righteousness: Abraham's trust in God's promise	❏
Day 4	Romans 5–8; Galatians 5:13-25	Reconciliation with God; freedom in the Spirit	❏
Day 5	Romans 9–11	God's faithfulness to Israel	❏
Day 6	Covenant Meditation on Galatians 3:23-29	All are one in Christ Jesus.	❏
Day 7	Group Meeting Experience with Romans 14:1–15:2	Practicing grace	❏

Episode 6

Day 1	Hebrews 1–2; Psalm 8	Praise for God's Son	❏
Day 2	Hebrews 3–4; Numbers 14	Faithfulness and loyalty	❏
Day 3	Hebrews 4:14–7:28; Psalm 110	Jesus is our covenant mediator.	❏
Day 4	Hebrews 8:1–10:18; Leviticus 16	Jesus grants us entrance to the most holy place.	❏
Day 5	Hebrews 10:19–13:25	Faith hall of fame	❏
Day 6	Covenant Meditation on Hebrews 6:10-11	Grateful love serves.	❏
Day 7	Group Meeting Experience with Hebrews 5:11–6:12	Honor	❏

Episode 7

Day 1	1 Corinthians 1–4	Immature boasting	❑
Day 2	1 Corinthians 7–10	My freedom is good, but it's not always good for others.	❑
Day 3	1 Corinthians 11–14	No person is better than another.	❑
Day 4	1 Corinthians 15; 2 Corinthians 1:1-11; 4–6	Our faith is pointless without Christ's resurrection.	❑
Day 5	1 Corinthians 16; 2 Corinthians 7–9	Cheerful generosity	❑
Day 6	Covenant Meditation on 2 Corinthians 4:7-12	God will rescue us.	❑
Day 7	Group Meeting Experience with 1 Corinthians 13:4-8	Love never fails.	❑

Episode 8

Day 1	Deuteronomy 5–9	The Ten Commandments and the greatest commandment	❑
Day 2	Deuteronomy 29–32	Old and new covenants	❑
Day 3	Joshua 1–2; 23–24	Moses reinvented	❑
Day 4	Judges 1–2; 19–21	Downward spiral	❑
Day 5	1 Samuel 13–15; 28:3-25	Tragedy of King Saul	❑
Day 6	Covenant Meditation on Deuteronomy 6:4-9	Renewing the covenant	❑
Day 7	Group Meeting Experience with Deuteronomy 6:1-19	A portrait of the covenant	❑

Episode 9

Day 1	Ruth 1–2	Famine, loss, and exile	❑
Day 2	Ruth 3–4	Redemption and restoration	❑
Day 3	Esther 1–4	Plot	❑
Day 4	Esther 5–8	Counterplot	❑
Day 5	Song of Songs 1–2; 4:1-7; 5:10-16	Love unplugged	❑
Day 6	Covenant Meditation on Song of Songs 8:6-7a	God loves you.	❑
Day 7	Group Meeting Experience with Ruth 1:8-18	Solemn promise for life	❑

Episode 10

Day 1	Luke 1:1–4:30	Jesus fulfills hopes and confounds expectations.	❏
Day 2	Luke 10:25-37; 13; 15; 16:19–17:19; 18:1-17; 19:1-10	Jesus proclaims God's kingdom.	❏
Day 3	Luke 22–24	Jesus, the rejected prophet, dies and rises again.	❏
Day 4	Acts 1–4	Jesus' followers receive power from the Holy Spirit.	❏
Day 5	Acts 8:1b–11:18	Unlikely newcomers join the church.	❏
Day 6	Covenant Meditation on Acts 2:42-47	Teaching, prayers, and shared meals	❏
Day 7	Group Meeting Experience with Luke 4:14-30	Jesus preaches in his synagogue.	❏

Episode 11

Day 1	2 Samuel 7; 9; 11–12	David's use and abuse of power	❏
Day 2	1 Kings 11–13	Loss of Israel	❏
Day 3	1 Kings 17–19; 21	King versus prophet	❏
Day 4	2 Kings 17–19	The fall of Samaria and the northern kingdom	❏
Day 5	2 Kings 22–25	The fall of Jerusalem and the southern kingdom	❏
Day 6	Covenant Meditation on 2 Kings 5:1-14	Who is the leader?	❏
Day 7	Group Meeting Experience with 2 Samuel 7:1-17	Covenant with David	❏

Episode 12

Day 1	1 Thessalonians 1–5	Encouragement for faithful living	❏
Day 2	2 Thessalonians 1–3	Harassed	❏
Day 3	1 Timothy 1:1-2; 2–4; 6:1-2, 11-15	Discernment	❏
Day 4	2 Timothy 1–4	An ethical will	❏
Day 5	Titus 1–3	Baptism and the Holy Spirit fuel faithful living.	❏
Day 6	Covenant Meditation on 2 Timothy 3:14-17	Scripture is useful.	❏
Day 7	Group Meeting Experience with 1 Thessalonians 1:2-10	Thanksgiving	❏

Episode 13

Day 1	Proverbs 1–4	Learning discernment	❑
Day 2	Proverbs 10–15	Speaking the truth	❑
Day 3	Proverbs 25–29	Using power and influence wisely	❑
Day 4	Ecclesiastes 1–4	When life seems pointless	❑
Day 5	Ecclesiastes 9–12	Everyday moments of joy	❑
Day 6	Covenant Meditation on Ecclesiastes 3:1-8	What is good for my life?	❑
Day 7	Group Meeting Experience with Proverbs 2:1-19	How to become wise	❑

Episode 14

Day 1	Philemon	Reconciliation of "brothers"	❑
Day 2	Philippians 1–4	Reconciliation and the fellowship of believers	❑
Day 3	Colossians 1:1–3:17	Reconciliation as the hidden treasure of God	❑
Day 4	Ephesians 1:1–5:20	Reconciliation as the cosmic reality	❑
Day 5	Colossians 3:18–4:1; Ephesians 5:21–6:9	A reconciled household	❑
Day 6	Covenant Meditation on Philemon 1:4-7	Reconciled in Christ	❑
Day 7	Group Meeting Experience with Ephesians 2	From death to reconciled life	❑

Episode 15

Day 1	James 1–2	Faith and impartiality	❑
Day 2	James 3–5	Penitence and patience	❑
Day 3	1 Peter 1:3–4:11	New life guided by Christ	❑
Day 4	1 Peter 4:12–5:14	Waiting for the last days	❑
Day 5	Jude and 2 Peter	When the great day is delayed	❑
Day 6	Covenant Meditation on James 1:22-26	Doers of the word	❑
Day 7	Group Meeting Experience with 1 Peter 2:4-10	Chosen people	❑

Episode 16

Day 1	Isaiah 1; 5:1–7:17; 9:2-7; 11:1-10	Royal prophet	❏
Day 2	Hosea 1:1-9; 2; 11:1-9	How can I give you up, Ephraim?	❏
Day 3	Amos 1:1–3:8; 5; 7:10-17	A lion has roared.	❏
Day 4	Micah 1:1–3:12; 6:1-8	What the Lord requires from you	❏
Day 5	Zephaniah 1; 3; Malachi 3–4	The great day of the Lord is near.	❏
Day 6	Covenant Meditation on Micah 6:8	Justice, love, and humility	❏
Day 7	Group Meeting Experience with Amos 5:7-24	Seek good.	❏

Episode 17

Day 1	John 1:1-18; 3–4	God's children love the light.	❏
Day 2	John 5; 9; 11	From healing to discipleship	❏
Day 3	John 14–17	So that they will be made perfectly one	❏
Day 4	John 18–21	Resurrection community	❏
Day 5	1 John 2–4; 2 John; 3 John	Hospitality is Christian love in action.	❏
Day 6	Covenant Meditation on John 15:9-13	Living well for others	❏
Day 7	Group Meeting Experience with John 13:1-17	Foot washing	❏

Episode 18

Day 1	Psalms 1–2; 19; 119:1-42	God's expectations	❏
Day 2	Psalms 13; 22; 80; 90	Desperate prayer for help	❏
Day 3	Psalms 34; 107; 116; 138	Giving thanks	❏
Day 4	Psalms 8; 104; 148	Creation songs	❏
Day 5	Psalms 146–150	Hallelujah!	❏
Day 6	Covenant Meditation on Psalm 139:1-6	Lord, you know me.	❏
Day 7	Group Meeting Experience with Psalm 42	Like a deer that craves streams of water	❏

Episode 19

Day 1	Job 1–2	Job's story	☐
Day 2	Job 3; 9; 19; 31	Job's response	☐
Day 3	Job 4–5; 8; 11	The friends' arguments	☐
Day 4	Job 38–41	God's speeches from the whirlwind	☐
Day 5	Job 42; reread Job 1–2	Job's response to God and the epilogue	☐
Day 6	Covenant Meditation on Job 2	What do you say to a friend in pain?	☐
Day 7	Group Meeting Experience with Job 42:7-17	Double for his trouble?	☐

Episode 20

Day 1	Jeremiah 1–4	Jeremiah's call and Judah's disregard of the covenant	☐
Day 2	Jeremiah 27–29	Living under Babylonian rule	☐
Day 3	Jeremiah 16; 18–20	Jeremiah's lament for himself and for his people	☐
Day 4	Lamentations 1–2; 5	The people's call for help	☐
Day 5	Ezekiel 34–37	Ezekiel's visions of transformation; a new covenant	☐
Day 6	Covenant Meditation on Lamentations 3:1-24	Living with crisis	☐
Day 7	Group Meeting Experience with Jeremiah 31:15-34	The new covenant	☐

Episode 21

Day 1	Isaiah 40–43	Creation	☐
Day 2	Isaiah 49:1–52:12	Comfort	☐
Day 3	Isaiah 52:13–55:13	Restoration	☐
Day 4	Isaiah 56:1-8; 58–61	Justice	☐
Day 5	Isaiah 63:7–66:24	Presence	☐
Day 6	Covenant Meditation on Isaiah 43:1-7	Hope comes from God.	☐
Day 7	Group Meeting Experience with Isaiah 40:12-31	God as creator of the world and of Israel	☐

Episode 22

Day 1	1 Chronicles 10:1–11:9; 28–29	The temple at the center of the community	❑
Day 2	2 Chronicles 33–36	Return and restoration	❑
Day 3	Ezra 1; 2:68–6:22	Rebuilding	❑
Day 4	Ezra 7–10	Ezra continues the restoration.	❑
Day 5	Nehemiah 1–2; 4; 7:73b–8:18	Nehemiah rebuilds walls; Ezra renews the covenant.	❑
Day 6	Covenant Meditation on 2 Chronicles 15:12-15	Don't abandon each other!	❑
Day 7	Group Meeting Experience with 1 Chronicles 29:10-19	David's prayer	❑

Episode 23

Day 1	Daniel 1–2	The emperor's dream	❑
Day 2	Daniel 3–4	The emperor's madness	❑
Day 3	Daniel 6	Civil disobedience	❑
Day 4	Daniel 7	Fifth monarchy	❑
Day 5	Daniel 9	Daniel's prayer	❑
Day 6	Covenant Meditation on Daniel 9:4-19	Trusting the covenant	❑
Day 7	Group Meeting Experience with Daniel 11:27-35	What about apocalyptic visions?	❑

Episode 24

Day 1	Revelation 1–3	John is called.	❑
Day 2	Revelation 4:1–8:1	Opening the scroll	❑
Day 3	Revelation 12–14	Defeating evil	❑
Day 4	Revelation 15–17	Seven plagues	❑
Day 5	Revelation 19–22	Final destination	❑
Day 6	Covenant Meditation on Revelation 7:9-17	Making us new	❑
Day 7	Group Meeting Experience	Our covenant	❑

COVENANT
Leader Guide

COVENANT
Leader Guide

BASIC NEEDS OF A COVENANT GROUP

HOW TO USE THIS LEADER GUIDE

Welcome to the Covenant Bible Study! As a facilitator, you play a key role in the weekly group meeting experience, which is a critical component of Covenant. Your guidance will shape the interactions between participants and nurture the impact the Bible has on their lives. The group meeting experience can form close covenant relationships among others. These relationships are just as important as the human transformation that comes from studying the whole scope of the Bible.

HOW TO USE THE GROUP AND LEADER HELPS

Your group can enhance the Covenant experience by taking advantage of online helps at the website—CovenantBibleStudy.com. Tell the participants in your group about it. All other Covenant materials are available in print or digital format.

Participants may purchase the interactive Covenant app for mobile devices, such as those supported by Apple or Android. A participant can respond to readings by journaling in the app, reading the assigned scriptures, and viewing videos. Optionally, participants can download and listen to the daily Bible readings, which are excerpted from the audio edition of the Common English Bible. A digital edition of the *CEB Study Bible* is also available for purchase through this app. Highly motivated participants can subscribe online to additional Bible reference tools.

When leaders register their groups online, they can communicate with participants about meeting reminders and offer other guidance for their Covenant experience together. This group tool can also send a daily e-mail to each participant with the text of that day's Bible reading. Ask the participants to record the e-mail addresses of other group members in their participant guides. Also record the participants' e-mail addresses in this leader guide so you can communicate with them about meetings and about any joys or concerns for the group.

Each participant has three types of essential needs. To ensure a fruitful, healthy group meeting experience for participants, pay attention to these basic necessities:

PHYSICAL NEEDS: "Am I safe and comfortable?"

People have fundamental physical needs that must be addressed for them to maintain focus and attention. To meet these needs, ensure the following:

1. Temperature: Set the thermostat in the room at a comfortable level.
2. Comfort: Allow food, drinks, bathroom breaks, and time to stand up and stretch.
3. Punctuality: Honor the time participants are devoting to the study by starting and ending each session promptly. When time is up, even if it is in the middle of a conversation, give people permission to leave if they need to, being particularly attentive to child-care needs and nursery volunteers.
4. Minimal distractions: Reduce distracting outside noises. Invite people to silence their cell phones at the start of each session and to refrain from texting.

EMOTIONAL NEEDS: "Who is around me? Can I trust them?"

For people to feel fully secure, they need to be comfortable with those around them. To meet these needs, ensure the following:

1. Names: Learn people's names right away, say them often, and welcome people personally when they arrive. Provide name tags for the first few episodes.
2. Chairs: Arrange the chairs in the room to suggest equality (no chairs higher, more comfortable, or more prominently placed than others).
3. Prayer: Pray for participants, even (and especially) before they meet for the first time. Always allow time for sharing joys and concerns at the beginning or conclusion of each session, and encourage people to share the task of offering the closing prayer.
4. Confidentiality: Remind people often that what is shared during each group meeting experience must be kept within the group.
5. Healthy disagreement: It is likely that people will offer contradictory points of view. Don't shy away from conflict, as sometimes those discussions will elicit opportunities for growth. However, don't let those disagreements become personal.

MENTAL NEEDS: "Why am I here? What's the point?"

Finally, people need to know that the time they invest in this experience will be well spent. To be certain they can gauge the merits and progress of this process, ensure the following:

1. Main point: For each episode, share with the group the main points that will direct their time and energies.
2. Preparation: Be an example of the benefits that come from being prepared. Read all the material in advance, and keep the discussions moving forward.

3. Questions: Carefully construct the questions you will ask the group to discuss, and tailor them to the interests and dynamics of the group. Use open-ended questions that require more than simple responses from participants.
4. Listen: Though you are a participant and are free to offer your own insights, show what healthy conversation looks like by being a good listener. The ideal ratio of talking/listening for a facilitator is 20/80.
5. Enthusiasm: Share your excitement and encourage participation by completing all the assigned work yourself.

HELPFUL HINTS

Because every group is composed of unique people, your Covenant group may have its own particular set of dynamics and challenges. The following are some tips to help your group succeed:

The best time to meet: The publisher has carefully tested in-depth Bible study dynamics with more than two million participants over twenty-five years. This kind of in-depth experience for Covenant will require approximately ninety minutes for the group to reconnect, discuss, view the video, and pray together. It's tempting to schedule the Covenant group meeting on a Sunday morning during an education hour, before or after worship, but it's unusual for a church to allow more than forty-five or fifty minutes for a typical Sunday school experience. Covenant Bible Study is an in-depth, small-group experience with a daily Bible reading discipline, and successful groups of this kind usually meet on a Sunday evening or on a weeknight to allow for a comfortable bond among the participants. Covenant Bible Study is also formatted in eight-week modules to give the group flexibility in scheduling around holidays or vacations.

The ideal class size: A group of eight to twelve people is an ideal size. Classes that are larger than twelve make it too easy for people to feel anonymous and even miss classes without being noticed. Large groups also take longer to form the kinds of relationships that are critical to meaningful Bible study. Groups smaller than eight, on the other hand, can lack the kind of diversity of background and opinion that enhance and motivate the richness of the experience.

What to do when a participant talks too much: When you sense that someone is commanding too much of the discussion, carefully determine whether that person is being a detriment to the group process. Some people have personalities that necessitate speaking in order to think. But if you discern that correction is necessary for the benefit of the group, first try some nonverbal cues. Avoid making eye contact with that person when you ask a question of the group, or break participants up into smaller discussion groups in order to minimize the person's effect on the whole group. Also try some verbal cues: Remind people after you ask certain questions to keep answers brief, or ask other people in the group for their responses. Of course, if necessary, address the concern privately with an individual outside the meeting, thanking this person for their contributions and asking for assistance in eliciting discussion from others in the group.

What to do when a participant talks too little: Some individuals require time to process their own thoughts before they verbalize them. Others are more introverted, shying away from talking in front of a group. Again, use eye contact, looking directly at those who appear reluctant to talk. Breaking the group into pairs encourages all participants to share their opinions. Do refrain, however, from putting people on the spot. No one should feel coerced into speaking when he or she is uncomfortable. And when quieter people do choose to speak their thoughts in front of the whole group, praise them for their contribution without sounding patronizing.

Don't be afraid of silence: Sometimes when you ask a question, there will be prolonged periods of silence in the group. You will be tempted to interrupt that silence with your own answers and insights, to move quickly to another question, or to call out people directly for their responses. Instead, feel free to sit in that silence, trusting that people are sorting out their own answers and struggling in a healthy way. Rather than breaking that silence with your own answers, a good alternative is to break the participants into smaller groups to discuss the question, making it less threatening for folks to develop their own responses verbally.

Stay on track: Inevitably, topics of conversation will emerge from your group that aren't central to the main points of the session. Use your best judgment in discerning which discussions are more diversionary and less helpful. Gently return the conversation back to the central ideas, and if need be, offer opportunities for interested folks to continue other conversations after the meeting.

Watch for participants who listen well and would make good discussion facilitators. Provide opportunities for them to lead, and give them any discussion questions and materials (DVD, leader guide) at least a week in advance. They will make great substitutes if you must miss a week.

THE ROLE OF FACILITATOR

You don't need to be a formally trained biblical scholar to succeed as a facilitator. You need only the following attributes to do your work well:

Be a learner: You are a participant too on this journey. As you read the daily scriptures and participant guide material, you will be tempted to do so exclusively through the lens of a facilitator. Instead, allow yourself to be as transformed and inspired by these sacred texts as you hope participants will be. Cultivate a curiosity and openness to meanings that are important to you, and others will draw from your enthusiasm.

Be a tour guide: You don't need to be a resident expert on every biblical and theological matter that your group will discuss. Instead, like a docent in a museum, your job is to direct their attention to aspects of the Bible and the Christian faith that are important for them to notice. You will guide conversations with provided structured questions designed to draw their interest and elicit their input.

Be prepared: The success of the group experience is directly related to your level of preparedness before each session. By using the materials in this leader guide, familiarize yourself with the learning objectives and key concepts for each week, carefully craft the questions that will spur conversation in your group, and structure the meeting time and setting to stimulate the best learning, devotion, and relevance to life.

Be attentive to stories: There's an easy tendency in a Bible study like this one to get completely caught up in the intellectual conversations about theology and biblical interpretation. Sometimes, however, the most effective way to deepen our understanding is through storytelling. Allow and encourage people to tell their own stories, modeling for them the power of storytelling by being vulnerable enough to do it yourself.

> **Tip:** To stimulate stories in the group, master storyteller Michael Williams offers retellings of ten biblical stories, which are available by download from CovenantBibleStudy.com. These stories are linked in the episodes where they fit.

Remember that a key to your group's success will be in training people to listen to stories—not only the stories they share with others but the grand, unfolding story of God's love found in scripture.

> **Tip:** An additional video for leaders on how to prepare for the group meeting experience at the last minute is available for download at CovenantBibleStudy.com. You can also find other helpful videos for leaders at the website.

PARTICIPANT GUIDE 1
EPISODE 1—Creating the Covenant
RELATIONSHIPS
Reading the Bible to live and love well

EXPECTATIONS FOR THE COVENANT EXPERIENCE

During the first group meeting experience (Episode 1), you should try to accomplish the following things:

1. Give the participants a taste of the Covenant group experience.
2. Explain why covenant is a very important concept and pattern throughout the Bible.
3. Establish the expectations for the group: regular attendance, confidentiality, and respect for each other in conversation.
4. Show the brief orientation video presented by the cohosts.
5. Explain how to use the episodes in each participant guide and how they establish a daily and weekly rhythm for in-depth Bible study.
6. Talk briefly about the parts of a study Bible (table of contents, maps, notes, and so on) and other tools for Bible study (concordance, Bible dictionary, *CEB Gospel Parallels*). Direct participants to CovenantBibleStudy.com for other reliable online resources for Bible study.
7. Explain that you are signing up the group at CovenantBibleStudy.com to receive daily readings, calendar information, and more via e-mail. You will need each participant's e-mail address to register the group. Encourage participants with mobile devices to visit the website and find direction on where to purchase the Covenant Bible Study app. They can view the participant guides digitally within the app. Other digital tools can be purchased there as well.
8. Collect contact information for each participant (and have the group record e-mail addresses and phone numbers in their participant guides). Discuss child-care needs, transportation concerns, and so on.
9. Pray for each other.

Materials needed: *Covenant Leader Guide*; participant guides; *Creating the Covenant* DVD (or video download); extra pens or pencils; name tags; a scrapbook or family photo album; a story or memory from your own family's past that locates and somehow defines who you are

....

Optional: Have your group read Deuteronomy 10 before this first session (or budget time to read it in the group meeting). Find more online resources, including additional video content, at CovenantBibleStudy.com.

THE GOAL AND SCOPE OF COVENANT BIBLE STUDY

This Covenant experience will guide participants in a comprehensive, in-depth study of the Bible over the next several months. Unlike the learning participants may have experienced in other groups, this in-depth study of the whole Bible emphasizes the biblical concept of *covenant* as a unifying pattern through all the books in the Old and New Testaments. It underscores the unique relationship that God chooses to have with us as God's people. This relationship is grounded in the faithfulness of God's love and in our ongoing commitment to stay in love with God while we share signs of that love with others.

Each episode connects to an aspect of this covenant relationship, which is summarized in the heading of each participant guide:

Creating the Covenant: The first participant guide explores in eight episodes how a biblical covenant is created and established. It covers the stories about our origins in Genesis, the critical Exodus narrative about the freedom of God's people, the stories of a new teacher in the Gospels of Matthew and Mark, and other biblical books that highlight foundational aspects of Christian belief and practice.

Living the Covenant: This participant guide builds on the concept of covenant by applying it to actual relationships in everyday life. The books included in this set of eight episodes are instructive, such as the accounts of emerging leadership problems first among the tribal chieftains, and then among the kings and prophets. It presents the spiritual and political crises that formed the early church; it searches for practical wisdom in the teachings of Israel's sages; and it considers the practical guidance found in Paul's letters as the emerging church learned how people of very different cultures can join together in a common mission.

Trusting the Covenant: This final participant guide tackles the loss of hope, which is restored by faithfulness in the midst of suffering. It explores the many ways that the biblical narrative encourages commitment to God when it is unreasonable and costly. The compelling story of Job, the stirring prophetic oracles during the Hebrew exile, and the imaginative symbolism of apocalyptic literature challenge and encourage us to faithful living.

During this first meeting, pass out participant guides (or point to the digital equivalent), and ask your group to open them. They should fully read Episode 1 (the overview) and Episode 2 (Torah: Genesis) before the next meeting.

> **Tip:** Have participants pay for their materials (guides, study Bibles, meditations) at the first session. Some groups prefer to circulate a weekly envelope so participants can pay later (or even pay a little at a time, depending on your church's reimbursement policy or budget). Some participants, of course, may purchase the Covenant app on their mobile devices.

Point out these features:

1. Notice the three distinct participant guides. There are three guides because some groups will meet for eight weeks, take a break, and then meet for the next set of episodes. A cautious participant may limit her investment to an eight-week experience, though the life-giving relationships formed in the group will usually draw reluctant participants into the full transforming experience.

2. Open the first guide, *Creating the Covenant*, and look at Episode 2 together. Describe the rhythm of the daily readings.

3. Note the title (Torah: Genesis), episode theme (Who Are We?), learning objective (Creating covenants with God and others), list of daily Bible Readings, and "Our Longing for Relationship." Highlight the Covenant Prayer section where they will read aloud the prayers and scripture passages at the beginning of the session. Explain that the space between each prayer and scripture is for writing down individuals who come to mind as needing prayer. Let the participants know you will write down prayer concerns at the end of their session each week.

4. Point out the genre and scripture book introductions (such as Torah and Genesis) that participants will read on Day 1 each week. Emphasize that each daily scripture reading includes questions for thoughtful reflection. They will want to write any questions they have about the reading in the shaded area beside each reading summary. These questions and thoughts will stimulate group discussion at the weekly group meeting where the group will study a particular passage together.

5. Describe the Covenant Meditation exercise on Day 6 and how it may occasionally be done with the group in the weekly meeting.

6. The last section is the Group Meeting Experience discussed below.

7. Mention that in addition to the participant guides, each person should obtain a study Bible. The *CEB Study Bible* is preferred. The digital edition of the *CEB Study Bible* is also available for purchase in the Covenant mobile app. Other study Bibles are acceptable too, but trying a new study Bible that participants haven't used before will likely awaken fresh meaning. The notations in the *CEB Study Bible* will answer most questions or trigger new ones while the participant reads a biblical passage.

THE GROUP MEETING EXPERIENCE

Each *Covenant Bible Study* episode follows the same essential structure by balancing conversational teaching from biblical experts with engaging discussion among the participants. *Covenant* is designed so that the meaning of the Bible isn't found in merely listening to a biblical scholar or listening to one's own inner voice. Only through conversation in community, in the Covenant group meeting experience, can we discover the Bible's transformative power. During some weeks the group might be so full of energy and questions that conversation leaves less time for the video. That's okay. The spiritual energy that wakes up and transforms a life is the most important result from this kind of Bible study.

The structure of the *Covenant Leader Guide* is designed to create options for facilitators so the weekly group experience creates an encounter with scripture that changes lives. You will discover in the coming weeks what strategies work best in your group. There is often more to do in the leader guide than your group has time to accomplish in one sitting. Schedule a break in your group meetings (for a stretch or restroom break). Whether your group meets for seventy-five minutes or two hours (ninety minutes is the sweet spot), you can try each section in the leader guide during the first few weeks and see what works best with your group. Meet at the same time each week if at all possible.

1. GATHERING TOGETHER (10 min.)

The opening questions of this segment in each episode are designed to prompt conversation on a general topic that connects to the main theme of the episode. Begin by reading the scriptures in the Covenant Prayer section for Episode 1. Have one person say the phrase, "For those who . . . ," and then the whole group responds by reading the scripture passage aloud (Neh 8:8 and then 8:10).

At this first meeting, ask the participants to think about a close personal relationship. The relationship might be with another human being, or it might be with an animal such as a dog or cat. Make a list of the relationships treasured in the group. In a column next to the list, write down the feelings that these relationships produce (e.g., contentment, anxiety, joy, avoidance, anger, safety, and so forth). Encourage someone to explain their feelings about this relationship through a story or anecdote. It might be a love story, or perhaps it comes from remembering a parent. (Examples: the day my dad taught me to drive; when my mom helped me shop for a prom dress; when my best friend introduced me to my future husband; when my brother wrecked my car.)

Ask the participants to reflect on why personal relationships with others and with God are important. (Answers might include: preventing loneliness, overcoming selfishness, managing appetites, sharing, forgiving wrongs, providing patience, humility, caregiving, children, and so forth.)

2. REFLECTING TOGETHER (10 min.)

This segment guides participants to share what they learned from the week's scripture readings with questions that tie their discoveries into a central theme. The study also encourages participants to memorize and share verses from the readings that they found particularly meaningful.

In the first participant guide, we establish the purpose of covenant in the Bible. The covenants are based on memories of God's promises to the families of Noah, Abraham, Moses, David, and Jesus. Give participants a few minutes to scan over the section in Episode 1 titled "Life that Fits and Connects." Memories of divine promise are based on retelling stories, much as we retell a story by means of a scrapbook.

Bring a scrapbook or family photo album to the first group meeting (and consider asking participants in advance to bring one too). Ask the participants to describe how their families preserve and remember ancestors and relatives. Ask for stories, and be prepared to tell a memory from your own family's past that locates and defines who you are, or perhaps that defines the hope and expectation you have for future generations. (Here is an example of a fruitful response: "After our parents divorced, my sister and I moved with my mom from California to North Carolina, where we started at a new school in a very different culture. I found that being the new kid was tough, but it also gave me a reboot on my self-image, and I have used that skill to restart my life several times over the years.")

> The optional Tips sections offer leader reminders and practical suggestions for improving your Covenant group experience as a facilitator.

3. VIDEO SEGMENT (25 min.)

Play the orientation video for Episode 1. The cohosts for this opening conversation are Rev. Shane Stanford, Senior Pastor at Christ United Methodist Church in Memphis, Tennessee; and Rev. Christine Chakoian, Senior Pastor at First Presbyterian Church in Lake Forest, Illinois. They will meet with a different biblical scholar in each video episode.

Each video in the coming weeks features a conversation between the hosts and a biblical scholar around the Covenant table. Their conversation is a model for the kind of learning dynamic that is central to this study. The questions in this section of the leader guide can be used at the conclusion of the video to prompt participants to reflect on the scholar's words in the context of their own discoveries. Encourage them to write down their own questions while they watch the video.

TAKE A BREAK (10 min. optional)

Never underestimate the power of a well-placed break! Participants come back better able to focus and learn if they stretch, take a bathroom break, and talk to each other outside of the formal discussion. Be strict about time, though. Whether it's five or ten minutes, choose a time for breaks that works best with your group. Offline conversations and interactions with the group are key to your success as a group leader. The relationships you strengthen during these breaks are as important as any of the biblical ideas discussed.

4. DISCOVERING TOGETHER (15 min.)

This segment in the following episodes builds on the insights of the biblical scholar and analyzes a single passage from the week's readings. The questions in the Group Meeting Experience sections of the participant guide encourage a comprehensive look at the form, style, and central meaning of the scripture text. This segment will teach participants how to "go deeper" in the way they explore the Bible's meaning.

If you handed out the participant guides before the first meeting, or if individuals downloaded the participant guides to their mobile devices, assign a single Bible passage (Deut 10) to be read before the meeting. It will be discussed briefly at the first meeting during this segment. Alternatively, if you wait for the first meeting, read Deuteronomy 10 aloud together, taking turns. Then ask the participants to separate into two groups and discuss by using the following questions:

1. How does the story in Deuteronomy 10 build on the story of the two stone tablets in Exodus 24:12-18? What did Moses do with those tablets? Why are the tablets still needed?
2. The covenant chest (called an "ark" in the KJV) is a container for God's presence, and the two tablets are a reminder of God's ten important expectations. Ask the two groups of participants to make a list of ten expectations they have for their closest personal relationship.

Bring the whole group together and discuss how committed relationships are based in faithful love and mutual responsibility. Be sensitive to those who have been hurt by broken relationships or betrayals, and explain how scripture can guide us through forgiveness and reconciliation from painful experiences in our pasts.

5. CENTERING TOGETHER (10 min. optional)

This segment provides a meditation, which is a devotional way to read the Bible. This is a critical part of the experience because it ensures that the study experience is not only informative for the mind but also formative for the heart. It will teach participants how to use imagination, prayer, and listening while reading scripture. These spiritual practices can strengthen their relationships with God. You may choose to have willing participants report on this experience (always located on Day 6 in the participant guide) if they are trying it at home. As an alternative, the leader guide includes this as a weekly group practice every week because some individuals are unfamiliar with this kind of meditation. Decide the best fit for your group. Try it both ways, as individuals and as a group.

An additional book of Covenant Meditations (sixty-six distinct meditations, one per book in the Bible) is available for participants who find this type of scripture reading practice enriching. Here is an example from Ezekiel 36 in *Covenant Meditations*:

A new heart

When I make myself holy among you in their sight, I will take you from the nations, I will gather you from all the countries, and I will bring you to your own fertile land. I will sprinkle clean water on you, and you will be cleansed of all your pollution. I will cleanse you of all your idols. I will give you a new heart and put a new spirit in you. I will remove your stony heart from your body and replace it with a living one.

Ezekiel 36:23c-26

Praying the word

At times our hearts harden. We become stubborn toward other people, different opinions and points of view, situations that make us uncomfortable, and even toward ourselves. After reading this scripture passage, sit quietly and reflect on the last time you felt your heart harden—or become "stony"—toward someone or something. What was happening at the time? Why did you respond with a stubborn heart? What would it take for your heart to soften again toward this person or circumstance? Offer a prayer that God might help your heart come alive again toward whatever caused your heart to become stony.

6. SERVING TOGETHER (5 min.)

Read together the "Signs of Faithful Love" at the end of this episode. Then remind group members that they are committing to a twenty-four-week Covenant experience together where they will:

- read the Bible daily and write responses in their participant guides;
- pray for other members of the group each day;
- meet with the group every week;
- listen for God speaking through the Bible and each other; and
- invite the Holy Spirit to change their lives through exposure to the good news of salvation through the faithfulness of Jesus Christ, who is encountered in the scriptures.

Participants are encouraged to conceive and share *tangible* ways that each week's readings will alter their priorities and perspectives and shape their behavior. Most vital Covenant groups will mature to the point where they put their faith into practice over twenty-four weeks. A well-balanced learning experience gives weight to piety (reading scripture, prayer, Christian conversation) as well as mercy (tangible signs of faithful love in the community).

Ask group participants who are willing to share how each has volunteered to serve or to help others in the past. Make a list of the tangible things they have done for others, and affirm the scope and range of their experiences. (Some examples may include: mowing an aging neighbor's lawn as they recover from surgery; mission trips to build housing for impoverished families at home or abroad; repairing playground equipment at a local park; providing transportation to doctor visits for those who no longer drive; tutoring second graders in basic math at a local elementary school; honoring first responders; and so on.) More examples of concrete things your group can do together or individually are found at CovenantBibleStudy.com.

7. NEXT WEEK (5 min.)

If there's anything the group needs to know about the next week's meeting (location change, a break before starting a new participant guide, extra supplies for the meeting), be sure to notify everyone as the group meeting experience is winding down. Also take this opportunity to introduce the next week's theme and to encourage participants to choose a verse to memorize and share at the following meeting. Be sure to mention that there are additional videos available at CovenantBibleStudy.com for participants who want to enhance their study throughout the week.

8. CLOSING PRAYER (5 min.)

Each session closes with a time for sharing prayer requests and concerns with each other. Encourage participants to write down each other's needs (in the next episode of their participant guides) and remember them each day in the upcoming week. Point out the particular concern for individuals who are struggling to find themselves, to know who they are or where they belong. Ask them to write these requests under the Covenant Prayer segment for Episode 2.

Finally, be sure to draw the group's attention again to "Our Longing for Relationship" at the beginning of each episode and "Signs of Faithful Love" at the end of each episode—at the times designated in the leader guide. These handles serve as helpful starting and ending markers for your group discussion, moving participants from positions of marginal commitment to high commitment in their path toward discipleship.

PARTICIPANT GUIDE 1

EPISODE 2—Torah: Genesis

WHO ARE WE?

Creating covenants with God and others

The book of Genesis begins with the wide-angle view of God's love—love for all creation—and gradually zooms in to the love that shapes our relationships with each other. The daily readings from this week sequentially follow that progression:

Day 1: beginning with creation;
Day 2: Noah, Babel, and the human community;
Day 3: Abraham and the establishment of nationhood;
Day 4: Jacob and the Israelite community; and
Day 5: family and kinship ties.

Each level of magnification has a unique way of supporting the overall theme of Genesis: God's loving relationship with all of life and our call to be in loving relationships with God and each other.

This episode will help your group:

- become familiar with the important biblical concept of covenant;
- discover how relationships in community can be broken and then restored through God's love; and
- identify the different voices that tell the stories of Genesis.

Materials needed: *Covenant Leader Guide*; *Creating the Covenant* participant guides; *CEB Study Bible*; *Creating the Covenant* DVD (or video download); extra pens or pencils

Optional: An additional video on the tower of Babel and the unique role of Israel is available for download from CovenantBibleStudy.com, as well as a video retelling the story of Abraham, Sarah, and the three visitors.

1. GATHERING TOGETHER (10 min.)

Genesis uses ancestral stories to give meaning to community and to our relationship to God and the wider world. After the opening Covenant Prayer, divide participants into pairs and invite them to share any stories they can think of that have been significant in shaping their family origins and their own identities. For example, to where does your family (birth or adopted) trace its origin, and what are the earliest stories you know about ancestors? How did your childhood experience in your family shape who you are today? Where does your name come from?

If participants prefer, they can also share stories related to any community to which they belong: their churches, their neighborhoods, or their countries. How do these stories reveal insights into the characters and identities of the participants' particular communities?

> **Tip:** Before your group arrives, preview and test the DVD or video download on the television or computer you will be using. Listen for anything that seems unclear to you or challenging to your group's presuppositions about the Bible or about Genesis.

2. REFLECTING TOGETHER (10 min.)

Read together "Our Longing for Relationship" at the beginning of the episode. Invite participants to break up into pairs and share any passages from the week's readings that were particularly meaningful to them, along with any insights they received from the readings. They might also share any verses they chose to memorize for the week.

pg 22

Read together the second paragraph of the introductory essay "Torah," and remind participants that the purpose of covenant is to explain:

- the purpose of a community;
- our relationship with God; and
- our role in the larger world.

By using those three criteria, invite them to analyze the scripture readings from the week.

Divide participants into two groups, and have each group look more closely at the two main covenants introduced in this episode: (1) Noah in Genesis 9:1-17 (God's covenant with all of life); and (2) Abraham in Genesis 15 and 17 (God's covenant to form a great nation). For each passage, have the group members answer these questions:

1. What does this story tell us about God's expectations for the community?
2. What is God's desired relationship to this community?
3. What is the role that God calls this community to have with the outside world?

Each of these stories also contains evidence that human communities often fall short of God's intent and become broken. Keeping the same two groups, have one group look more closely at the stories of Noah (Gen 6:5-22) and Babel (Gen 11:1-9), and have the other group look at the story of Joseph (Gen 37 and 45). For each story, have participants answer these questions:

1. What is the threat facing God's community in this story?
2. Where do you see evidence of God's love at work to restore community in this story?
3. How are the people in this story called to be part of the solution?

3. VIDEO SEGMENT (25 min.)

The video for Episode 2, on the DVD or available by download, allows the group to overhear a conversation with Theodore Hiebert, who is Professor of Old Testament at McCormick Theological Seminary in Chicago, Illinois. Before showing the video, ask the participants to listen for one or more of the following conversation points:

1. The book of Genesis is more than a book of beginnings; it answers the deepest human questions about who we are in the scheme of things. It's about where we fit and what our responsibilities are as members of the human community and the broader community of life.
2. Family is the biggest and deepest influence on the understanding of covenant relationships in Genesis. The family relationships that define covenant for these writers are understood in terms of gift (it chose us, we didn't choose it) and responsibility (there is a fitting way to respond).
3. The family/covenant relationships of Genesis are characterized by sibling rivalry, conflict, and the ever-present danger that the family will disintegrate. While wrong decisions and disobedience define the human characters from the first age (and beyond), these decisions are always about relationships: choosing for or against the relationship. However, with the exception of the brothers Cain and Abel, the family of Abraham finds a way to resolve differences through forgiveness and generosity.
4. God's hand is seen in these stories as the power that works toward keeping all things together. God also calls privilege and authority into question by leveling the playing field on behalf of women, second sons, and others diminished by the dominant culture.

At the end of the viewing, ask the group members one or two of the questions below:

1. Did you grow up hearing any stories of how your "tribe" came to be a family? How did your parents or grandparents (or even great-grandparents) meet? Was there doubt or peril that put your family tree in danger? Do you define who you are (and where you fit) more in terms of family relationships or something else (career, friendship groups, college sorority/fraternity, church, and so on)?
2. How or in what ways is your family a gift to you? What are the house rules or basic responsibilities that come with being part of a family (a daughter, son, sister, brother, mother, father, aunt, uncle, cousin, godparent)?
3. The Genesis families are plagued by rivalry and conflict. Can you think of any famous family rifts that didn't end well? What about in your own family? What role has forgiveness or generosity played in healing these family conflicts? Who has been Esau to Jacob (or Joseph to his brothers) in your clan?

TAKE A BREAK (10 min. optional)

Learn something about someone in the group that you didn't already know.

4. DISCOVERING TOGETHER (15 min.)

Break the participants into two subgroups and invite them to work with the Group Meeting Experience from Genesis 9:7-17 outlined in their participant guides.

5. CENTERING TOGETHER (10 min. optional)

Genesis reminds us that we are created in God's image and therefore have the same kind of imaginative capacity as the God who envisioned creation out of chaos. Reading the scriptures with our imaginations can therefore be an exercise of divine creativity, and it is an effective way to engage the stories of the Bible. Lead the participants through the Covenant Meditation on Genesis 1:26-31 found in their participant guides.

6. SERVING TOGETHER (5 min.)

Read together the "Signs of Faithful Love" at the end of the episode, then break the participants into pairs. Have them review for a moment any notes they recorded and any insights they gained related to the human responsibility of restoring broken communities back to God's loving intent. Just as the flow of the Genesis stories suggests, those responsibilities can range from the global (our responsibility to the environment and the whole created world) to our personal relationships with others (family and community). Have them share with each other how they feel called to particular service this week.

7. NEXT WEEK (5 min.)

Turn to Episode 3 and briefly introduce next week's title and theme. Encourage participants to select a verse from the readings that they might commit to memory and share next week. Be sure to mention that there are additional videos available at CovenantBibleStudy.com for participants who want to enhance their study throughout the week.

8. CLOSING PRAYER (5 min.)

Ask for any prayer concerns or joys, and invite participants to write these items down in the space provided under next week's Covenant Prayer. This way, the prayer needs will be in front of them as they read throughout the week. Close in a prayer together.

PARTICIPANT GUIDE 1

EPISODE 3—Exodus, Leviticus, Numbers

FREEDOM AND INSTRUCTION

Privileges and responsibilities of the covenant

The texts for this week summarize one of the most foundational narratives in the biblical faith: the liberation of God's people from oppression and the promise of freedom. The readings track:

Day 1: the call of Moses;
Day 2: the journey into the wilderness;
Day 3: the establishment of the Sinai covenant;
Day 4: the instructions for holy living; and
Day 5: trust in the future.

This episode will help your group:

- review the essential elements of the exodus narrative;
- explore the ways that the Torah instructs the people of God for righteous living; and
- renew together a commitment to faithfulness in covenant community.

Materials needed: *Covenant Leader Guide*; *Creating the Covenant* participant guides; *CEB Study Bible*; *Creating the Covenant* DVD (or video download); extra pens or pencils

Optional: An additional video on Moses and the name of God is available for download from CovenantBibleStudy.com.

1. GATHERING TOGETHER (10 min.)

Read the Covenant Prayer together. Jewish people understand the purpose of the Torah as instructive: It teaches people how to live holy lives in the context of community relationships. Invite participants to together on the question: "Who taught you how to live a holy life?" Ask them to name specific people — variety of influences: parents, family members, church members, and others. Remind them that such spiritual formation best occurs in our relationships with others.

> **Tip:** Israel has a life with God. We read about it to discover our own lives with God. You will help your group understand life with God this week through Bible study.

2. REFLECTING TOGETHER (10 min.)

Read together "Our Longing for Relationship" at the beginning of Episode 3 in the participant guide. Invite participants to break up into pairs and share any passages from the week's readings that were particularly meaningful. Specifically, have them explore the question: "What did you learn about the function of the Torah in the life of faith?" Have them share any insights they gained from the questions in the daily readings section of their participant guides. They might also share any verses they chose to memorize for the week.

The readings from Days 1 and 2 retrace the familiar narratives of Moses and the liberation of the Israelites from oppression under Pharaoh. Divide the participants into groups of two or three and have each group make two lists based on the first two days' readings:

1. how Moses and the people of God were in need; and
2. how God responded to their various needs with power and provision.

Have them report their lists to the whole group.

The readings from Days 3 and 4 explore the responsibilities now expected from the liberated people as a result of their covenant relationship with God. By maintaining the same subgroups, invite participants to list all the responsibilities for holy living from the selected passages in Exodus and Leviticus. Have them report their lists to the whole group.

Finally, as a whole group, consider together the reading from Day 5 in Numbers. Ask group members to reflect on the question: "What difference does it make to you that many of the positive outcomes of your faithfulness today may not be realized by people until long into the future?"

3. VIDEO SEGMENT (25 min.)

The video for Episode 3, on the DVD or available by download, allows the group to overhear a conversation with Alejandro F. Botta, who is Associate Professor of Hebrew Bible at Boston University. Before showing the video, ask the participants to listen for one of the following important points:

1. Passover celebrates the story of Israel's liberation from captivity in Egypt, but it is bittersweet because of the tragic, high cost of convincing Pharaoh to set the people free.
2. The God of the Bible relates to people (individuals and the community) through covenants. The covenant at Sinai is for the creation of a people and nation with all the instructions and expectations

required to live in harmony with each other. Like the US Constitution, ongoing interpretation and amendments for changing situations are required when applying these teachings in the lives of real people (for example, fairness and justice).

3. God is holy, and holiness defines the covenant people as a special and distinct community. They are set apart and defined by the expectations that make faithfulness to God's justice a priority, opposing any society governed by a covenant of death.

4. Moses is the paradigm and pattern for a prophet, but four key women made his success possible: Shiphrah and Puah (midwives), Miriam (his sister), and Bithiah (daughter of Pharaoh). He enjoyed the benefits of the highest culture in the world, yet something in his heart made him give up everything in Egypt and answer God's call to go on an unknown journey for the people.

At the end of the viewing, ask participants one or two of the questions below:

1. Freedom is difficult and costly. It seems that it is almost always won at a great price from those who have a vested interest in the enslavement of others. What are some hard-won freedoms we celebrate today? Does the cost of freedom make it bittersweet? What people still await freedom from captivity? If God is a God who sets the captive free, what role can covenant people play in the ongoing work of liberation in the world?

2. Most of us have requirements that keep our homes and communities in order. Think of teachings from your childhood, or even your grandparents' time, that have been modified or changed over the years in your family. Has this been in the direction of more or less freedom for people in the house? Are there rules we outgrow? What are some of the behaviors that define your family or friends as the people they are known to be (honesty, work ethic, dress, habits)?

3. Moses forfeits a life of privilege for the sake of others' salvation and freedom. This story is central in the Jewish and Christian traditions. What aspects of his life do you find admirable? What makes him a problematic hero? How is he like us? How do we wish to be like Moses?

TAKE A BREAK (10 min. optional)

Find group members willing to help you connect with participants when they miss a week.

4. DISCOVERING TOGETHER (15 min.)

The Ten Commandments are an essential part of faithful living. They remind us of the responsibilities inherent to being in covenant relationships with God and each other. Lead the group in a discussion of the five questions about Exodus 20:1-17 in the Group Meeting Experience portion of their participant guides, asking for any new insights they have gained about the Ten Commandments.

5. CENTERING TOGETHER (10 min. optional)

We often have the tendency to perceive the Holiness Codes of Leviticus as either too dry or too irrelevant. To remind us that following these commandments was and is foremost a spiritual practice, the Covenant Meditation on Leviticus 19:1-2 draws participants into an experience of what it means to be holy. Guide the group in this exercise, leaving enough time for them to share insights and impressions with each other.

6. SERVING TOGETHER (5 min.)

Read together the "Signs of Faithful Love" at the end of the episode. Break the participants into pairs, and have them review for a moment any notes they recorded and any insights they gained throughout this episode. Invite them to share specific ways that they will renew their commitments to faithful (and holy) living this week.

7. NEXT WEEK (5 min.)

Turn to Episode 4 and briefly introduce next week's title and theme. Encourage participants to select a verse from the readings that they might commit to memory and share next week. Be sure to mention that there are additional videos available at CovenantBibleStudy.com for participants who want to enhance their study throughout the week.

8. CLOSING PRAYER (5 min.)

Ask for any prayer concerns or joys, and invite participants to write these items down in the space provided under next week's Covenant Prayer. This way, the prayer needs will be in front of them as they read throughout the week. Close in a prayer together.

PARTICIPANT GUIDE 1

EPISODE 4—Gospels: Matthew and Mark

GOD'S KINGDOM

Jesus reveals instructions for a new covenant community.

The word *kingdom* can seem antiquated, detached from contemporary political and social realities. However, the word is the New Testament way of describing our covenant relationship with the Lord, who sets expectations and responsibilities for every part of Christian life. Jesus talked publicly about God's kingdom, or the kingdom of heaven, more than any other subject. This week's readings from Matthew and Mark are filled with instances when Jesus used parables to reveal the mysteries of God's kingdom (Days 1, 2, 4, and 5), and when he encouraged people to live a life in contrast to the kingdoms or empires of this world (Day 3).

This episode will help your group:

- study the ways that Jesus used parables to reveal aspects of God's kingdom;
- explore the sermon on the mountain in Matthew to discover how Jesus defined faithful living; and
- commit to reorienting their lives according to the ways of the kingdom.

> **Materials needed:** *Covenant Leader Guide*; *Creating the Covenant* participant guides; *CEB Study Bible*; *Creating the Covenant* DVD (or video download); extra pens or pencils
>
> **Optional:** An additional video on the parables of Jesus is available for download from CovenantBibleStudy.com.

1. GATHERING TOGETHER (10 min.)

Invite participants to share instances when their Christian convictions were hard to maintain in the face of the culture around them. When has following Jesus been difficult for them? Encourage them to share not only the times when they successfully upheld their Christian commitments, but also the times when they didn't succeed. Be sure to preserve an environment of understanding, forgiveness, and confidentiality for those who wish to share such experiences. Pray the Covenant Prayer from the participant guide.

2. REFLECTING TOGETHER (10 min.)

Read together "Our Longing for Relationship" at the beginning of Episode 4 in the participant guide. Invite participants to break up into pairs and share any passages from the week's readings that were particularly meaningful. Specifically, have them explore the question: "What words from Jesus did you find especially challenging this week?" Have them share any insights they gained from the questions in the daily readings section of their participant guides. They might also share any verses they chose to memorize for the week.

Jesus called his followers to perceive the world in a way that was contrary to the lens of the Roman establishment. Their perspectives, priorities, and motivations were to be grounded in faithfulness to God, rather than in the political and social structures of the surrounding culture. To reveal these intricate mysteries, Jesus spoke in numerous parables, many of which were covered in this week's readings. Divide the class into four groups, and invite each subgroup to select a parable from one of the following daily readings:

Day 1: Mark 1–4 (parables of the soils, the lamps, and the seed)
Day 2: Mark 12–14 (parables of the tenant farmers and the fig tree)
Day 4: Matthew 11–13 (parables of the soils, the weeds, the mustard seed,
the treasure, the merchant, and the net)
Day 5: Matthew 18–22 (parables of the lost sheep, the unforgiving servant,
and the workers in the vineyard)

For each parable selected, invite them to share how the parable describes the differences between God's kingdom and the world's empires.

The reading from Day 3 is the famous sermon on the mountain, in which Jesus (the new Moses) teaches specific ways that Christians are to live in contrast to the cultures around them. Keeping the same four groups, have each one consider a different chapter from Matthew 4–7. Have each group make a list of the kinds of qualities Jesus commands that are countercultural to the world. After the groups have shared their lists with everyone, have them reflect on which instructions seem the most difficult to follow.

> **Tip:** Check how the group is keeping up with the daily readings. Invite participants to share strategies for getting them done (audio Bible, reading the daily e-mails from CovenantBibleStudy.com, a special "quiet time" each day, and so on).

3. VIDEO SEGMENT (25 min.)

The video for Episode 4, on the DVD or available by download, allows the group to overhear a conversation with Stephanie B. Crowder, who teaches at McCormick Theological Seminary in Chicago, Illinois. Before showing the video, ask the participants to listen for one or two of these key conversation points:

1. Gospels are similar to Greco-Roman biographies. They give accurate accounts of what matters most in a life. A biography shows what goes on in the "dash" between the birth and death of its subject. (For example, a dash goes on a tombstone: born 1908–died 1992.) Similar to the tension between biography and memoir, gospels work to communicate the turning points that matter most in their portrayal of a life affected by others.

2. Matthew and Mark present the Jesus story in unique orders that reflect what they are trying to say to their particular Christian communities.

3. Mark writes to a mostly Gentile community suffering greatly during the social and political unrest of the first Jewish-Roman war (65–70 CE). He paints a picture of Jesus, the Human One (or "Son of Man" in the KJV), who suffers just as the people are suffering, and who declares God's reign that counters and upends the order of the Roman Empire.

4. Matthew is written to a primarily Jewish community of believers after the destruction of the temple (85 CE), showing Jesus as a new Teacher who embodies the covenant promise and invites his followers to live as heirs of the covenant.

After the video, ask participants one of the following questions:

1. Recall some version of the Jesus story from your childhood or youth (Sunday school flannel boards, film strips, animated videos on VHS, sermons, or a children's Bible). What did you think about Jesus? Do you recall pictures or paintings of Jesus from your past? How is he presented? How does Mark's story of the Human One who preaches God's kingdom versus Caesar's kingdom fit with that picture? Does Jesus seem to change as you read these good news biographies more closely?

2. How would Jesus' message of a countercultural kingdom be received today in places where power and prestige are wielded (Wall Street; Washington, DC; or Silicon Valley)? How do we typically respond to prophets and preachers who say a reversal of privilege and power is in order?

3. Think of a teacher or mentor (or author) whose message wisely steered you or someone you know in the right direction. What gives power and credibility to a new teacher's message? If a teacher could heal the sick, would that change your perspective on their message? Who do you know that needs the healing touch of Jesus this week? What if he touched you today?

TAKE A BREAK (10 min. optional)

Take a moment to see whether a well-prepared person in the group might be willing to lead a part of the discussion for a future meeting.

4. DISCOVERING TOGETHER (15 min.)

The Group Meeting Experience on Matthew 9:18-33 focuses on the very important miracle stories in Matthew's Gospel. In these miracles, Jesus is the new Moses, the new Teacher, who establishes his authority as the deliverer (the Christ, or Messiah) of God's people. When Jesus restores life to the dead daughter of the Roman commander, Jesus demonstrates that even the Roman authorities recognize God's power. Yet even before that happens, when Jesus heals the untouchable, unclean woman with a bleeding disorder, he demonstrates to the Jewish leaders that his power is available to the person with the least status among them.

Divide the participants into two groups. Have one group discuss questions 1–4 about the authority of Jesus to deliver individuals from death or suffering regardless of their social statuses. Have the other group discuss question 5 concerning their views of how and when Jesus relieves our human suffering now. Report back to the whole group.

5. CENTERING TOGETHER (10 min. optional)

The Covenant Meditation exercise this week is a familiar passage to those who believe that children have a special place and proximity to Jesus in the kingdom (Mark 10:13-16). Ask participants who are willing to share any thoughts or insights that came out of their prayerful reading of this passage.

6. SERVING TOGETHER (5 min.)

Read together the "Signs of Faithful Love" at the end of the episode. Break the participants into pairs, and have them review for a moment any notes they recorded and any insights they gained throughout this episode. Invite them to consider how they are specifically challenged to change their perspectives, motives, and behaviors to be more in line with God's kingdom (or covenant).

7. NEXT WEEK (5 min.)

Turn to Episode 5 and briefly introduce next week's title and theme. Encourage participants to select a verse from the readings that they might commit to memory and share next week.

8. CLOSING PRAYER (5 min.)

Ask for any prayer concerns or joys, and invite participants to write these items down in the space provided under next week's Covenant Prayer. This way, the prayer needs will be in front of them as they read throughout the week. Close in a prayer together.

PARTICIPANT GUIDE 1

EPISODE 5—Letters: Romans and Galatians

GRACE

Trusting that the faithfulness of Jesus is enough

In the letters to the Galatians and to the Romans, Paul offers his most comprehensive views about the gospel of Jesus Christ and the nature of salvation. This week's readings summarize:

Day 1: Paul's understanding of the need for salvation;
Day 2: the sufficiency of Christ's faithfulness for salvation;
Day 3: trusting in the promise of salvation;
Day 4: the tangible results of salvation; and
Day 5: how salvation is offered to everyone, Jew or Gentile.

This episode will help your group:

• explore the nature of sin and our need for God's grace;

• analyze the nuances of Paul's doctrine of salvation; and

• apply Paul's theology in tangible ways to share God's grace with others.

Materials needed: *Covenant Leader Guide*; *Creating the Covenant* participant guides; *CEB Study Bible*; *Creating the Covenant* DVD (or video download); extra pens or pencils

1. GATHERING TOGETHER (10 min.)

Paul is very clear about the nature of God's grace: It's a free gift, undeserved and unmerited, for which no work is necessary. After praying the Covenant Prayer from the participant guide, invite the participants to think about a time they received a gift they didn't deserve, for which they couldn't possibly repay the giver. Expand their thinking beyond tangible presents to include acts of kindness, valuable insights, and transformative experiences. How does one's feeling of indebtedness impact one's gratitude to the giver of the gift?

> **Tip:** Effective group leaders understand that their job is to love Covenant group participants by listening to their lives and appreciating what God is doing in them.

2. REFLECTING TOGETHER (10 min.)

Read together "Our Longing for Relationship" at the beginning of Episode 5 in the participant guide. Invite participants to break up into pairs and share any passages from the week's readings that were particularly meaningful. Specifically, have them explore the question: "Did you understand anything new this week about the nature of God's grace?" Have them share any insights they gained from the questions in the daily readings section of their participant guides. They might also share any verses they chose to memorize for the week.

Implied in each of this week's readings is Paul's understanding of the human condition: Human beings are selfish and sinful. By using insights from the daily scripture texts, invite the group to reflect together on the nature of sin. How does Paul define sin? How does Paul make the argument that everyone is a sinner? Have them construct a succinct definition of sin.

When describing sin and how God overcomes it, Paul depicts theological tensions, each of which is reflected in the daily readings. Divide the group into four subgroups, inviting them to analyze one of the following polarities from the daily readings. Have them explore how Paul finds a "middle way" between these diametrically opposed ideas:

Day 1: God's justice vs. God's faithfulness
Day 2: Law (Torah) versus grace
Day 4: Old self versus new self
Day 5: Salvation for Gentiles versus salvation for Jews

Invite participants to report their conclusions with the rest of the group.

3. VIDEO SEGMENT (25 min.)

The video for Episode 5, on the DVD or available by download, allows the group to overhear a conversation with Diane Grace Chen, who is Associate Professor of New Testament at Palmer Theological Seminary in King of Prussia, Pennsylvania. Before showing the video, ask the participants to listen for one of the following important points:

1. Letters represented Paul and substituted for his presence in the churches he founded and loved. While they are often concerned with putting out fires, Paul's letters usually represent his attempt to guide churches from a pastoral perspective, stressing some of the same big ideas that are always front and center for him: grace, Law, salvation, and freedom in the Spirit. It is the grace of salvation through the faithfulness of Jesus Christ that Paul desperately wants the people to remember.

2. Paul seems to be really angry in his letter to the Galatians. Some leaders have tried to supplement the faithful work of Jesus by imposing circumcision as a required mark for belonging to God's covenant family. For Paul, Jews are saved as Jews, Gentiles as Gentiles, and all of us only by God's grace through the faithfulness of Jesus. Trust in Jesus is enough. For Jewish Christians, circumcision is a sign or seal after the fact of faith. For Gentile Christians, the sign of baptism is enough.

3. The true mark of the community of faith is the presence of the Spirit that produces fruit, which are characteristics that help us maintain our relationships and be faithful to each other. The Spirit is a gift of grace that bears fruit in us, making us more gracious to ourselves and to others. The Spirit knows our weaknesses, and our challenge is to let go and trust that God will keep transforming us from within.

After the video, ask group members one or two of the following questions:

1. Recall the last time you received a stamped letter in the postal mail. Do you have any letters that you treasure? Can you hear the voice of the letter writer when you read their correspondence? When someone writes you a letter today, does it carry more or less weight (since there are so many other ways to communicate)?

2. What would your reaction be if someone told your close family members (children, siblings, parents, friends) that your love for them hinged on some achievement or favor they must perform? Does this example capture Paul's frustration with those who were trying to convince the Galatians to be circumcised? If trusting the faithfulness of Jesus on the cross is enough, why do some people add achievements to the list of requirements for receiving God's saving love?

3. Where do you see spiritual fruit in everyday life (see Gal 5:22-23 for a list of fruit)? How does reading the Bible help us understand what the Spirit wants us to do? What are some specific ways we can live by and follow the Spirit this week?

TAKE A BREAK (10 min. optional)

Use this time to thank a particular individual for a comment or insight shared.

4. DISCOVERING TOGETHER (15 min.)

Even though Romans is loaded with theological reasoning, the book concludes with some specific, practical guidance on how to live faithfully as a recipient of God's grace. Though the receipt of God's grace carries no qualification, it bears great responsibility. Invite someone to read aloud Romans 14:1–15:2. Then divide the participants into four groups, and have each subgroup study one of the questions in the Group Meeting Experience portion of the participant guide. Invite them to share their insights with the whole group.

5. CENTERING TOGETHER (10 min. optional)

The Covenant Meditation invites participants into a spiritual reading experience of Galatians 3:23-29, in which Paul affirms the work of God's grace to unify us and break down barriers of division. Lead participants in the exercise, then ask them to share ways that this text to the Galatians is meaningful to their own experiences.

6. SERVING TOGETHER (5 min.)

Read together the "Signs of Faithful Love" at the end of the episode. Break the participants into pairs, and have them review for a moment any notes they recorded and any insights they gained throughout this episode. Invite them to share specific ways that they will share God's grace with others.

7. NEXT WEEK (5 min.)

Turn to Episode 6 and briefly introduce next week's title and theme. Encourage participants to select a verse from the readings that they might commit to memory and share next week. Be sure to mention that there are additional videos available at CovenantBibleStudy.com for participants who want to enhance their study throughout the week.

8. CLOSING PRAYER (5 min.)

Ask for any prayer concerns or joys, and invite participants to write these items down in the space provided under next week's Covenant Prayer. This way, the prayer needs will be in front of them as they read throughout the week. Close in a prayer together.

PARTICIPANT GUIDE 1

EPISODE 6—Hebrews

WITNESS

Showing gratitude and loyalty to God

The book of Hebrews is the motivational speech of the New Testament. The readings for this week sample the flair and finesse of a skilled public speaker engaging an audience's imagination and calling them to a higher purpose. You may want to have many of these passages read out loud during today's session, to simulate the way in which the author intended these words to be experienced.

This episode will help your group:

- discover how the author of Hebrews develops a threefold argument for obedience to Jesus;
- make connections between the Hebrew audience and themselves to discover how they also can maintain their witness in the face of adversity, motivated by gratitude to Jesus Christ; and
- experience the words of Hebrews audibly, in the style in which they were originally intended.

Materials needed: *Covenant Leader Guide*; *Creating the Covenant* participant guides; *CEB Study Bible*; *Creating the Covenant* DVD (or video download); extra pens or pencils

Optional: An additional video on grace (and response) is available for download from CovenantBibleStudy.com.

1. GATHERING TOGETHER (10 min.)

After praying the Covenant Prayer from the participant guide, invite participants to pair with a partner and remember the greatest sermon, speech, or public address they ever heard. How did it inspire them, and what did it motivate them to do? What were the qualities of that speech that filled their minds (with information), stirred their hearts (with emotion), and provoked their behavior (with motivation)? What was the context at the time that speech was given that made delivering and hearing the speech so necessary?

2. REFLECTING TOGETHER (10 min.)

Read together "Our Longing for Relationship" at the beginning of the episode. Invite participants to break up into pairs and share any passages from the week's readings that were particularly meaningful to them, along with any insights they received from the readings. They might also share any verses they chose to memorize for the week.

Review together the three-part logic in the sermon from the Hebrews preacher:

1. the benefits that come to the person who puts their trust in Jesus;
2. the status and quality of Jesus, the giver; and
3. appropriate and inappropriate responses to Jesus' selfless generosity.

Those three ideas are reflected in the readings from the first three days. Combine pairs into three larger groups, and have each group look more closely at one of the first three daily readings.

Day 1: What are the qualities stated about Jesus that elevate him in honor and status?
Day 2: What benefits are promised to those who choose to maintain obedience to Jesus?
Day 3: What are the appropriate and inappropriate responses one can make to Jesus?

The author of Hebrews addresses a community tempted to waver in their firm commitment to Christ. In the most notable section of the book, the author offers a grand, sweeping review of biblical heroes who exemplify unfaltering commitment to God. As the contemporary audience of the Hebrews, how might we also be motivated by their example?

Divide the participants into two groups. Have one group analyze Hebrews 11 and make a list of the lessons we can learn from the historical figures contained in the chapter. Have the other group analyze Hebrews 12 and make a list of the appeals the author makes for the audience to maintain obedience to Christ. Have the groups then share their findings with each other, connecting how the author uses the historical illustrations in chapter 11 to support the specific appeals made in chapter 12.

> **Tip:** Perform gratitude by thanking group members who host, who provide food, or who help with setup and cleanup.

3. VIDEO SEGMENT (25 min.)

The video for Episode 6, on the DVD or available by download, allows the group to overhear a conversation with David A. deSilva, who is Professor of New Testament and Greek at Ashland Theological Seminary in Ashland, Ohio. Before showing the video, ask the participants to listen for one of the following key conversation points:

1. The book of Hebrews is a sermon written by an unknown author to an audience whose members are enduring a lot for answering God's call. The Hebrews are living with loss and tension with

those around them. Their neighbors either don't accept their commitments or perceive their confession of Christ as some kind of threat.

2. The dynamic concept of faith and discipleship in Hebrews uses metaphors like journey, race, and pilgrimage for a faith that is always on the move and ever at risk of distraction or falling away. The writer wants his hearers to respond with gratitude for all they have already been given in Jesus and with renewed energy for what God has done for them.

3. By using the rich image or lens of sacrifice from the Old Testament, the writer of Hebrews creates new ways of thinking about Jesus' death on the cross, his resurrection, and his ascension. He describes the work of Christ as a cosmic Day of Reconciliation that once and for all removes all obstacles to God's presence. By replacing fear with confidence, Jesus, our pioneer and forerunner, has made it possible for us to approach the holy with confident expectation of God's favor. We follow the "downward mobility" of so many people of faith from the Old Testament (and of Jesus himself) who exchanged privilege in this life for the promise that wherever God calls us to go is the right direction.

At the end of the viewing, ask the participants one or two of these questions:

1. Think of things that keep you from a closer relationship with someone you love (time, distractions, finances, busyness, broken promises, a past grudge or grievance, and so on). Who has the power to remove these obstacles? You? Them? What if everything that stood in the way of a better relationship was taken care of by an interested third party? What if Jesus has accomplished through his death, resurrection, and ascension an all-access pass to God, who calls us to a life of faithful love? How would life be different for you?

2. Can you think of a time when you or a friend were called to the principal's office to be reprimanded? Or perhaps when you were waiting to meet with a teacher, coach, manager, or supervisor? What was the waiting like? What did you (or your friend) expect to happen? How has Jesus removed fear from our relationship with God according to the writer of Hebrews?

3. Faith is to be sustained for the long haul in Hebrews. Think of something you have given up that was costly in the short run but that paid long-term dividends years later. How did you do it? What picture of future glory gave you strength to give up short-term satisfaction for the promise of something better later?

TAKE A BREAK (10 min. optional)
Take time to better know a quieter member of the group.

4. DISCOVERING TOGETHER (15 min.)

Hebrews 5:11–6:12 is loaded with energy as it reaches the high point of the author's speech. It is the heart of his argument, with even greater emotional appeal and rhetorical flourish.

Invite someone to read aloud Hebrews 5:11–6:12. Then divide the participants into five groups, and have each study one of the questions in the Group Meeting Experience portion of the participant guide. Invite them to share their insights with the whole group.

5. CENTERING TOGETHER (10 min. optional)

Much of the power of Hebrews is located in the audible experience of its words. Written manuscripts of speeches often fall short in capturing the passion and energy intended by the speaker. Lead the participants through the Covenant Meditation on Hebrews 6:10-11 found in their participant guides, and invite them to imagine hearing these words for the first time.

6. SERVING TOGETHER (5 min.)

Read together the "Signs of Faithful Love" at the end of the episode. Break the participants into pairs, and have them review for a moment any notes they recorded and any insights they gained related to (1) maintaining their witness in the face of the temptation to fall away; and (2) renewing a spirit of gratitude for the generous gifts Christ offers us. Encourage them to look for specific ways they will express both a renewed commitment to Christ and a renewed gratitude for God's blessings. Have them share with their partners the practical steps they will take this week.

7. NEXT WEEK (5 min.)

Turn to Episode 7 and briefly introduce next week's title and theme. Encourage participants to select a verse from the readings that they might commit to memory and share next week.

8. CLOSING PRAYER (5 min.)

Ask for any prayer concerns or joys, and invite participants to write these items down in the space provided under next week's Covenant Prayer. This way, the prayer needs will be in front of them as they read throughout the week. Close in a prayer together.

PARTICIPANT GUIDE 1

EPISODE 7—1 and 2 Corinthians

LOGIC OF THE CROSS

Consider what Christ accomplished.

One of the more admired characteristics of the Bible is its raw, unvarnished portrayal of humans and communities. The Bible doesn't sugarcoat the flaws and foibles of people. It showcases our selfishness and weaknesses as a way of convicting us of our own shortcomings. The letters of Paul to the Corinthian church are loaded with brutally honest assessments of a divided community that has lost its unity in exchange for hostile disagreements over matters both petty and pivotal.

This episode will help your group:

- explore the major areas of disagreement within the Corinthian church and assess the similarities between the Corinthians and the participants' congregations today;
- discover how Paul's emphasis on the cross offers an effective, albeit surprising, antidote to the church's poisonous divisions; and
- commit to specific ways that the love of God revealed in Christ can heal specific conflicts within the church.

> **Materials needed:** *Covenant Leader Guide*; *Creating the Covenant* participant guides; *CEB Study Bible*; *Creating the Covenant* DVD (or video download); extra pens or pencils

1. GATHERING TOGETHER (10 min.)

The population of the city of Corinth was among the most eclectic and diverse in the Roman world. After praying the Covenant Prayer from the participant guide, invite participants to list the various ways that their city or town is a diverse community. Encourage them to think about differences in ethnicity, socioeconomic status, religion, culture, entertainment, and other categories. How have these differences been problematic, as well as beneficial, to the strength of their communities?

2. REFLECTING TOGETHER (10 min.)

Read together "Our Longing for Relationship" at the beginning of Episode 7 in the participant guide. Invite participants to break up into pairs and share any passages from the week's readings that were particularly meaningful to them. Specifically, have group members explore the question: "What insights did you gain about the cross of Jesus and its ability to heal divisions?" Have them share any ideas they had from the questions in the daily readings section of their participant guides. They might also share any verses they chose to memorize for the week.

Invite the participants to divide into five groups to investigate each of the five daily readings. Specifically, have them look for the central issue or issues that were causing division within the Corinthian community. Invite them to name the issues and the corresponding verses that summarize the areas of disagreement. After all the groups have shared, invite them to reflect together on ways their churches also experience division over similar issues.

Paul suggests that the cross is the central solution to the tensions and divisions that exist within a faith community. It reorients our wayward perspectives and shatters presuppositions that contradict covenant community. Invite participants to reflect together about what the cross means. Ask them to describe a time when the cross was more than just a symbol to them. How did it change the way they saw themselves and their relationships with God and others? Next, break them up into groups of two or three and ask them to read 1 Corinthians 1:18-31. What does Paul say about the cross? How does he use the symbol of the cross to encourage people to set aside their selfishness and work toward harmony?

> **Tip:** Encourage your group to practice thinking about the logic of the cross whenever they see a cross used as decoration, as jewelry, or in architecture.

3. VIDEO SEGMENT (25 min.)

The video for Episode 7, on the DVD or available by download, allows the group to overhear a conversation with Monya A. Stubbs, a seminary professor who taught at Austin Presbyterian Theological Seminary in Austin, Texas. Before showing the video, ask the participants to listen for one of the following conversation points:

1. The letters to the church at Corinth show Paul addressing very concrete issues in a society organized by the patronage system of benefactors and clients, superiors and inferiors. This system stressed the pursuit of honor (for the elite) and tried to avoid shame (for inferior individuals). This mind-set valued the freedom of superiors to do whatever they wanted, and these behaviors subjected those of lesser value to whatever the dominant culture preferred.

2. Paul calls for this worldview and its way of doing things ("strongholds") to be brought under the mind of Christ. The mind of Christ is characterized by a different pattern, a logic of self-giving love, a logic of the cross, that trumps the logic of domination, patronage, and superiority.

3. The power and logic of love are applied to real-life problems in a way that balances the relationship between self and community. The freedom that comes with faith is qualified by the mind of Christ that always asks how my freedom will be beneficial to others.

At the end of the viewing, ask the participants one or two of the questions below:

1. We live in an age and culture where most of us think it is good to do (and get) what we want. Think of a time or a situation where someone's position or authority allowed that person to do things that offended or disregarded others in their sphere of influence. Was this person within their rights to behave that way? When has doing or getting what you want come with collateral damage for those close to you?

2. When have you seen someone, or even a group, apply the logic of the cross/the mind-set of Christ when it would have been easier to just do what they were free to do? Is this a conscious decision in each instance, or is the logic of love more like a habit formed, a way of life? Why do you think so?

3. Do you have a practical process for filtering choices or solving problems through the mind of Christ? If not, what might that look like (asking key questions about who will be affected, seeking wisdom from a mentor or the scriptures, praying for insight, and so on)?

TAKE A BREAK (10 min. optional)

During the break, ask another group member to lead one of the video discussion questions next week.

4. DISCOVERING TOGETHER (15 min.)

The Group Meeting Experience investigates the well-known "love chapter" from 1 Corinthians 13. Paul suggests that love expressed with mutual concern, rather than selfish desire, is a key to overcoming barriers and divisions within community. We are most familiar with hearing this passage in the context of wedding ceremonies, as guidance for marriage. But how might this text serve other kinds of human communities? Divide the participants into five groups to answer the five questions in the Group Meeting Experience. Invite them to share their conclusions with each other.

5. CENTERING TOGETHER (10 min. optional)

The Covenant Meditation invites participants into a spiritual reading experience of 2 Corinthians 4:7-12, which describes our lives as clay pots. Every one of us will be challenged to the breaking limit at times by suffering and death. But by following Jesus, who experienced death on the cross, new life is at work in us. Lead the group in the meditation, then ask participants to share ways that the analogy to clay pots is meaningful to their own experiences.

6. SERVING TOGETHER (5 min.)

Read together the "Signs of Faithful Love" at the end of the episode. Break the participants into pairs, and have them review for a moment any notes they recorded and any insights they gained throughout this episode. Invite them to share specific ways they will utilize both the gift of love and the power of the cross to overcome divisions within their community this week.

7. NEXT WEEK (5 min.)

Turn to Episode 8 and briefly introduce next week's title and theme. Suggest that participants select a verse from the readings that they might commit to memory and share next week. Be sure to mention that there are additional videos available at CovenantBibleStudy.com for participants who want to enhance their study throughout the week.

Encourage the participants to stay committed to their Covenant group relationships after the first milestone is reached with Episode 8. If you decide to take a break for a week or more after Episode 8, discuss with the group the date when you will start back up with the next participant guide: *Living the Covenant*. Be sure to update your group calendar at CovenantBibleStudy.com if you decide to take a break.

8. CLOSING PRAYER (5 min.)

Ask for any prayer concerns or joys, and invite participants to write these items down in the space provided under next week's Covenant Prayer. This way, the prayer needs will be in front of them as they read throughout the week. Close in a prayer together.

PARTICIPANT GUIDE 1

EPISODE 8—Deuteronomy, Joshua, Judges, 1 Samuel

COVENANT RENEWAL

Refreshing our relationships

It's clear by the episode title that this week's readings play a foundational role in our overall understanding of *covenant*. These readings reiterate and expand covenant loyalty:

Days 1 and 2: by the critical relationship that God has established with God's people in Deuteronomy;

Day 3: through the stories of inhabiting the promised land in Joshua;

Day 4: through the stories of official leaders and chieftains in Judges; and

Day 5: through the stories of the first prophet and first king in 1 Samuel, which outlines both the rewards and the consequences of obedience or disobedience to the covenant.

This week's episode will help your group:

- understand the ways that Deuteronomy illuminates the covenant established in Exodus;
- explore the ways that biblical figures embody different responses to the covenant; and
- renew their own commitments to keeping the covenant.

Materials needed: *Covenant Leader Guide*; *Creating the Covenant* participant guides; *CEB Study Bible*; *Creating the Covenant* DVD (or video download); extra pens or pencils

Optional: An additional video on the Moab covenant is available for download from CovenantBibleStudy.com, as well as one about teaching through story and interpreting the Ten Commandments. There is also a video retelling the story of Hannah and the infant Samuel.

1. GATHERING TOGETHER (10 min.)

In many ways, we are defined by the promises we intend to keep. Our commitments to our families, our jobs, our communities, our churches, and our country align our priorities and motivate our behaviors. After the Covenant Prayer, invite the group to name what promises undergird who they are. Have them reflect on the rewards of keeping those promises, including the positive influence doing so casts on those around them. Have them also reflect on the consequences of breaking those promises.

> **Tip:** Help your group watch for turning points in Israel's covenant life with God. These will resonate with turning points in their own lives.

2. REFLECTING TOGETHER (10 min.)

Read together "Our Longing for Relationship" at the beginning of Episode 8 in the participant guide. Invite participants to break up into pairs and share any passages from the week's readings that were particularly meaningful to them. Specifically, have group members explore the question: "What thoughts did you have this week about what it means to be a people who belong to God?" Have them share any insights they gained from the questions in the daily readings section of their participant guides. They might also share any verses they chose to memorize for the week.

As a whole group, invite the participants to come up with a brief statement summarizing the content of the covenant relationship described in Deuteronomy. What is the most succinct way to say (1) what God promises to the people; and (2) the responsibilities that the people must keep?

In the wake of Moses, a steady succession of biblical figures enters the picture, each embodying a distinct reaction to the command to keep the covenant. Have the group divide into subgroups, and have each one spend some moments reflecting on one of the following characters: Joshua, Deborah, Gideon, Samson, Jephthah, Samuel, and Saul. Have them identify what each figure said and did that indicates the extent of their commitment to the covenant. Invite participants to report their conclusions with the rest of the group.

3. VIDEO SEGMENT (25 min.)

The video for Episode 8, on the DVD or available by download, allows the group to overhear a conversation with Brent A. Strawn, who is Professor of Old Testament at Candler School of Theology in Atlanta, Georgia. Before showing the video, ask the participants to listen for one of the following conversation points:

1. Deuteronomy and the books that follow tell the story of how Israel became a people by re-creating God's Instruction in a new situation. Moses retells the story of the covenant to Israel in the new lands. Life in the land will be easier than Egypt, and the people will be tempted to forget their dependence on God, believing their prosperity is the work of their own hands. Moses preaches a

long sermon against any and all rivals to God (foreign gods, but also false hope in money, power, or military strength). He also restates the most important commandment ("no other gods") positively: You will love God with all your heart and strength.

2. Joshua tells the troubling story of Israel's conquest of the land of Canaan. The forces that must be vanquished in the land will be identified over time with more spiritual obstacles to covenant life. The language expressing God's anger with the Canaanites is applied to Israel itself, with God ultimately upset about disobedience and injustice.

3. In Judges and Samuel, the leadership cycle plays out with troubling repetition: People disobey/serve other gods; they are oppressed by their enemies; they cry to God for help; God hears and responds; tribal chieftains rescue them; and the cycle begins again, with God leaving them to their own devices. The unfaithful people—unruled by God or by a king—set up the monarchy when God raises up Samuel (last chieftain and first prophet), who will anoint Saul and David. Kings will be a problem, and prophets are there to keep them in line, but the real king missing in Israel is God.

At the end of the viewing, choose one of these questions to discuss:

1. Can you think of a time in your life when things were difficult financially, but when there followed an "upgrade," a move upward (across state lines, to a new hometown, a bigger house, a better job, or a higher standard of living)? The people of Israel are moving to a place with a store on every corner (full of milk and honey). When things are going well, do you have a difficult time trusting God? How can we love and trust God for bread one day at a time (as we do in the wilderness days) when we are living well in the land of milk and honey?

2. Is the "leadership cycle" familiar in your own life? Do you ignore God, get into trouble, cry for help, experience deliverance, change your life, and then repeat the cycle? How can God help you break this cycle? What do you need to do?

3. Prophets like Samuel (and Nathan) confront kings when their rule betrays covenant principles, especially the instruction about "no other gods." Is someone like Samuel or Nathan in your life to tell you tough truths when your priorities are out of touch with a God-first way of life? Why do we need these voices in our lives? How do they earn the right to tell us the truth?

TAKE A BREAK (10 min. optional)

During the break, look for someone who is stressed or having a difficult week, and let them know how much you appreciate their presence in the group.

4. DISCOVERING TOGETHER (15 min.)

The Group Meeting Experience takes a close look at Deuteronomy 6:1-19 by analyzing the way it clarifies and amplifies the Sinai covenant in the book of Exodus. Divide the participants into two groups, and have the first group answer questions 1–3 and the second group answer questions 4–6. After they have shared their responses with the whole group, have everyone discuss the final question, which asks us to think about keeping a covenant within our faith communities in today's world.

5. CENTERING TOGETHER (10 min. optional)

Remind the group that at its core, covenant is about relationship. It establishes a level of intimacy reserved between God and those privileged to be God's people. No study of covenant would be complete without inviting a personal encounter with God, allowing the words of scripture to draw a person into an experience of God's love. The Covenant Meditation exercise centers on Deuteronomy 6:4-9, following the practice of *lectio divina* (sacred reading). Lead the group in this exercise, allowing time for them to share their impressions with others.

6. SERVING TOGETHER (5 min.)

Read together the "Signs of Faithful Love" at the end of the episode. Break the participants into pairs, and have them review for a moment any notes they recorded and any insights they gained throughout this episode. Invite them to share specific ways that they will renew their commitment to keeping the covenant in every one of their relationships.

7. NEXT EIGHT WEEKS: *LIVING THE COVENANT* (5 min.)

Turn to Episode 9 in the *Living the Covenant* participant guide, and briefly introduce the title and theme. Encourage participants to select a verse from the readings that they might commit to memory and share when you next meet. Also mention that there are additional videos available at CovenantBibleStudy.com for participants who want to enhance their study of Ruth, Esther, and Song of Songs.

Celebrate the completion of the first eight episodes. Encourage the participants to stay committed to their Covenant group relationships now that the first milestone is reached with Episode 8. If you decide to take a break for a week or more after Episode 8, discuss with the group the date when you will start back up with the next participant guide: *Living the Covenant*. Be sure to update your group calendar at CovenantBibleStudy.com.

8. CLOSING PRAYER (5 min.)

Ask for any prayer concerns or joys, and invite participants to write these items down in the space provided under next week's Covenant Prayer (Episode 9 in the *Living the Covenant* participant guide). This way, the prayer needs will be in front of them as they read throughout the week. Close in a prayer together.

PARTICIPANT GUIDE 2

EPISODE 9—Ruth, Esther, Song of Songs

FAITHFUL LOVE

Committed relationships

Lest we think that the theology of covenant is an entirely cerebral enterprise, the stories of Ruth and Esther, and the poetry in the Song of Songs, remind us that covenant is primarily encountered through relationships. It connects us in a deeper way to God and to each other, strengthening bonds of trust and shaping the way we live. And just as with any relationship, covenant relationships are rooted in longing: a desire for unconditional love, intimacy, and fidelity. That desire is the foundation for all three books in this week's readings:

Days 1 and 2: a longing grounded in loyalty and obedience (Ruth);
Days 3 and 4: a longing conveyed through courage and self-sacrifice (Esther); and
Day 5: a longing expressed in passion and intimacy (Song of Songs).

This episode will help your group:

- recount the stories of Ruth and Esther and identify the ideals of faithful love contained in them;
- identify signs of faithful love contained in the poetry of Song of Songs; and
- discover ways to enhance their relationships with God through intimacy and obedience.

Materials needed: *Covenant Leader Guide*; *Living the Covenant* participant guides; *CEB Study Bible*; *Living the Covenant* DVD (or video download); extra pens or pencils

Optional: An additional video on Ruth and Esther is available for download from CovenantBibleStudy.com, as well as a video retelling the story of Ruth.

1. GATHERING TOGETHER (10 min.)

Given that human love in general, and marriage in particular, will be a recurring theme throughout this week's episode, recognize at the outset that participants will bring in a range of perspectives, history, and emotional attachments to the experience of human love in relationships. After the Covenant Prayer, invite participants to reflect on their own difficulties with human relational love for a few moments. In what ways do they experience relational love as a true reflection of God's love? How has it illuminated their relationships with God? How has it fallen short in their experiences of pain, betrayal, or resentment?

2. REFLECTING TOGETHER (10 min.)

Read together "Our Longing for Relationship" at the beginning of Episode 9 in the second participant guide. Invite participants to break up into pairs and share any passages from the week's readings that were particularly meaningful to them. Specifically, have group members explore the question: "What did you glean from these readings about both human love and divine love?" Have them share any insights they gained from the questions in the daily readings section of their participant guides. They might also share any verses they chose to memorize for the week.

Ruth and Esther are compelling stories of heroism, sacrifice, and loyalty. Break the participants into two groups, and invite each group to write a time line of major events in the plots of both Ruth and Esther (Days 1–4). For each main plot point, have them identify what a character's actions reveal about faithful love, both between human beings and between humanity and God. For example, one might say that Ruth's choice to stay with Naomi is an example of loyalty and fidelity, similar to God's faithfulness to us.

Next, divide the participants into four groups. Have each group take two chapters of Song of Songs (chapters 1–2; 3–4; 5–6; and 7–8). Invite them to make a list of all the verses that reveal longing and desire. For each verse, reflect on how one might apply the longing and desire in that verse to one's relationship with God. How might applying the verse in this way help us develop intimacy with God? Allow time for the groups to report their discoveries with everyone.

> **Tip:** Most of us have a story about a time when we chose to either identify with our tribe or leave it (like Esther). Remind your group that faithful love takes risks.

3. VIDEO SEGMENT (25 min.)

The video for Episode 9, on the DVD or available by download, allows the group to overhear a conversation with Judy Fentress-Williams, who is Professor of Old Testament at Virginia Theological Seminary in Alexandria, Virginia. Before showing the video, ask the participants to listen for one or more of the following important conversation points:

1. Ruth, Esther, and Song of Songs are part of the Jewish festival scroll and are linked to the Festival of Weeks (Shavuot), Purim, and Passover, respectively. Shavuot celebrates the giving of the Instruction (Torah) at Mount Sinai, which the people continue to receive. Esther is read during Purim to celebrate the people's rescue from Haman's treachery by Mordecai and Esther's risky faith. Song of Songs is read during Passover, celebrating Israel's liberation from Egypt.

2. The story of Ruth is a tale of identity and redemption where both Ruth and Boaz risk caring beyond the roles required of them. Ruth reveals a love motivated by more than contractual obligation, a faithfulness that is more than duty. Boaz takes a financial risk to redeem Ruth beyond the family obligations of levirate marriage (*levirate* means that the brother of a deceased man must marry the widow of the deceased man). Esther cleverly risks everything to identify with her people and rescue them from a genocidal plot.

3. Song of Songs puts passion and love on full display. It hints at a new creation where shame is banished, and it celebrates human love as a clue to grasping the intensity of God's longing and love for us. The passion of this "crazy love" is self-sacrificing, and it plants a seed of faithfulness that helped give rise to Israel's greatest king and led ultimately to the birth of our savior.

At the end of the viewing, choose one of the following questions to ask:

1. Think of a carol or song that brings back memories of Christmas from your childhood. What songs do you sing now to get in the mood for Advent or Christmas? Does your family read a certain book or poem, or do they tell the same story during this sacred season? Similarly, Ruth, Esther, and Song of Songs provide a sacred story and sound track for key Jewish festivals celebrating the remarkable gift of covenant love that the people must continue to receive.

2. Recall a time when you or a friend decided to take a risk for love. Has anyone ever had to take a chance on you (hire you, trust you with more responsibility, or put you in charge of something precious or costly)? What would you risk for the ones you cherish most?

3. Song of Songs uses words to fill the space of longing, to approximate what we miss when we can't be with ones we love. Can a song or story fill a space in our hearts when we're separated from someone we love? How about a yellow ribbon around a tree or a crooner's promise to "be seeing you in all the old familiar places"? Song of Songs is a duet that the singers must wait to sing together. It reminds us that love—God's and ours—is a longing that intensifies with waiting and celebrates with reunion. How will you wait for God's love this week?

TAKE A BREAK (10 min. optional)

Covenant living has a conversational sound track. During the break, listen for signs of group life: laughter, continued scripture discussion, casual sharing of struggles, or small celebrations.

4. DISCOVERING TOGETHER (15 min.)

The Group Meeting Experience investigates the beautiful and poignant exchange between Ruth and Naomi and elevates it as an example of true covenant fidelity. Invite the group to work in pairs on the Group Meeting Experience questions for Ruth 1:8-18, and then invite the whole group to share their conclusions with each other. How does the relationship between Ruth and Naomi exemplify our ideal relationship with God?

5. CENTERING TOGETHER (10 min. optional)

The Covenant Meditation for this week is immersed in Song of Songs 8:6-7a. Lead the group in this meditation as described in the participant guide. Help them articulate whether they sense and embrace God's love deeply and passionately. Explore how our memories and experiences of human love are connected to our perceptions of God's love in daily life.

6. SERVING TOGETHER (5 min.)

Read together the "Signs of Faithful Love" at the end of the episode. Break the participants into pairs, and have them review for a moment any notes they recorded and any insights they gained throughout this episode. Invite them to share how these insights will encourage them to pursue loyalty and intimacy in their relationships with God and fidelity in their relationships with others.

7. NEXT WEEK (5 min.)

Turn to Episode 10 and briefly introduce next week's title and theme. Encourage participants to select a verse from the readings that they might commit to memory and share next week. Be sure to mention that there are additional videos available at CovenantBibleStudy.com for participants who want to enhance their study throughout the week.

8. CLOSING PRAYER (5 min.)

Ask for any prayer concerns or joys, and invite participants to write these items down in the space provided under next week's Covenant Prayer. This way, the prayer needs will be in front of them as they read throughout the week. Close in a prayer together.

PARTICIPANT GUIDE 2
EPISODE 10—Luke and Acts
THE SPIRIT-LED COMMUNITY
To change our hearts and lives and tell others about it

The books of Luke and Acts form a continuous narrative about how the work of Jesus Christ and the Holy Spirit forms community and then expands it to include outsiders. Both books begin with a period of hopeful anticipation:

Day 1: the birth narratives of Jesus; and
Day 4: the expectation of the Holy Spirit.

Both books also include surprising notions of inclusivity as God's kingdom expands:

Day 2: to include outcasts; and
Day 5: to include outsiders.

But it is the death and resurrection of Jesus (Day 3) that serves as the critical pivot for the wider story. It is in the saving work of Jesus that the Christian community is shaped and conveyed to the outside world.

This episode will help your group:

- learn how Luke and Acts are intended to be read as one work;
- discover how the gospel often surprised unsuspecting people; and
- study instances in the life of Jesus and in the work of the Holy Spirit when the faithful community expanded to include people outside preconceived boundaries.

Materials needed: *Covenant Leader Guide*; *Living the Covenant* participant guides; *CEB Study Bible*; *Living the Covenant* DVD (or video download); extra pens or pencils

Optional: An additional video retelling the story of Peter and Cornelius is available for download from CovenantBibleStudy.com.

1. GATHERING TOGETHER (10 min.)

After the Covenant Prayer, invite participants to reflect on how they have experienced Jesus Christ in the context of their Christian communities. How has being part of a faithful community helped them become more like Jesus? Also, invite them to share their understandings of the Holy Spirit. What does the Holy Spirit mean to them, and how do they experience the Spirit? Remind them that throughout the New Testament, an experience of the Holy Spirit is rarely a private affair. The experiences occur in the context of community. How have they seen evidence of the Holy Spirit's activity in their communities?

> **Tip:** The dramatic displays of divine power get more attention in the Bible than God's constant life-giving presence. Look at the participants in your group and remember that God is powerfully present in their lives. Ask God to help you recognize that.

2. REFLECTING TOGETHER (10 min.)

Read together "Our Longing for Relationship" at the beginning of Episode 10 in the participant guide. Invite participants to break up into pairs and share any passages from the week's readings that were particularly meaningful to them. Specifically, have group members explore the question: "What did you discover about the work of Jesus Christ and the Holy Spirit in community?" Have them share any insights they gained from the questions in the daily readings section of their participant guides. They might also share any verses they chose to memorize for the week.

Luke and Acts contain examples of ways the good news came to some surprising people in unexpected ways. Have the group break up into four subgroups to take a look at the daily readings below:

Day 1: Zechariah, Elizabeth, and Mary
Day 2: The good Samaritan, the prodigal son, and Zacchaeus
Day 4: The people at Pentecost
Day 5: The Ethiopian, Saul, and Cornelius

For each reading, have them answer the following questions:

1. Who are the people who received a surprising word of good news?
2. After they were changed by the good news, how did they in turn positively influence the community around them?
3. Who might be the equivalent of these people in the community and the world today?

Next, invite the group to take a closer look together at the reading for Day 3. Invite someone to read aloud Luke 23:26-49. Note for the group that in Luke, even the crucifixion is experienced in the context of a community. Luke specifically names people who are present at the scene. Have the group make a list of those who witnessed the crucifixion (the crowds, the women, the criminals, the soldiers, the leaders, the centurion), and have them note the unexpected diversity of the people who were present. Of those people, whose lives were transformed (the criminal, the centurion)? Why might that detail be surprising to Luke's readers but in keeping with the overall theme of Luke and Acts?

3. VIDEO SEGMENT (25 min.)

The video for Episode 10, on the DVD or available by download, allows the group to overhear a conversation with Matthew L. Skinner, Associate Professor of New Testament at Luther Seminary in St. Paul, Minnesota. Before showing the video, ask the participants to listen for one of the following conversation points:

1. The Gospel of Luke and the book of Acts offer a vision of who God is and of what salvation means. Jesus is the fulfillment of God's intention for the world: to remake what it means to be a human being. The church continues Jesus' ministry in fellowship, feeding unlikely guests at the table, worship and prayer, discerning God's presence, healing, service, storytelling, witness, and mission.

2. Jesus is understood in Luke as a prophet who comes to: (a) reveal God's heart (what it looks like when God's desires are fulfilled in the world); (b) call people to changed hearts and lives (turning them toward outcasts and toward society's invisible people, where God is discovered); and (c) empower the church to carry on this prophetic role and identity in the world by the power and presence of the Holy Spirit.

3. The book of Acts kicks off with the story of Pentecost, where the promise of God's Spirit power comes to old and young, male and female, free and slave alike. This is (a) a call to belonging; and (b) a charge or call to ministry. The same things embodied by Jesus are to characterize the community gathered in his name—especially his welcoming of outsiders, who occupy a privileged place to encounter God's presence. The utterly unexpected welcome of Gentiles into the community with no conditions whatsoever was an unforeseen outcome that changed the whole course of (church) history.

After the video, choose one question below, or let the participants lead with a question they would have asked if they were sitting with Chris, Shane, and Matt at the Covenant table:

1. In Luke, where does Jesus see and show God at work? Ask participants to try this strategy for discerning God's presence: see, name, and tell. What keeps us from seeing God at work in regular life? Why are we sometimes afraid to name something as a God-sighting? What helps you recognize and respond to the Holy Spirit's work in your interactions with people on the outside of faith?

2. For Luke, the call to belong is also a call to care about the people who have captured God's heart. This is how we belong to God's covenant work of love. When has serving or helping others felt like a perfect fit to you? Are you still looking for that place where belonging and serving come together? (Optional: Ask the group to repeat this simple prayer this week: "I belong to God's love.")

TAKE A BREAK (10 min. optional)

Think about some of the great discussions your group has had to date. Compliment one of the participants for their crucial insight or contribution.

4. DISCOVERING TOGETHER (15 min.)

Jesus' hometown sermon in Luke 4:14-30 not only launches his public ministry but is a key thematic tie that unifies Luke and Acts. The Group Meeting Experience explores the ties between the Holy Spirit and Jesus' earthly ministry, and it reinforces Luke's emphasis on the impact the gospel has on people in community. Divide into four subgroups, and have each group discuss one of the four questions listed in the exercise. Have them share their discoveries with the whole group.

5. CENTERING TOGETHER (10 min. optional)

Acts 2:42-47 contains a vivid glimpse into the daily patterns of the early church. The Covenant Meditation invites an imaginative engagement with the text, immersing the reader into life as a first-century follower of Jesus. Lead the group through an experiential reading of the text. Invite the group to share their reflections, and encourage them to look for ways that their current faith community can better reflect the blueprint for church life advocated in the text.

6. SERVING TOGETHER (5 min.)

Read together the "Signs of Faithful Love" at the end of the episode. Break the participants into pairs, and have them review for a moment any notes they recorded and any insights they gained throughout this episode. Invite them to consider specific people who are outcasts and outsiders to their faith community and to share how they might expand the reach of the church to invite them in.

7. NEXT WEEK (5 min.)

Turn to Episode 11 and briefly introduce next week's title and theme. Encourage participants to select a verse from the readings that they might commit to memory and share next week. Be sure to mention that there are additional videos available at CovenantBibleStudy.com for participants who want to enhance their study throughout the week.

8. CLOSING PRAYER (5 min.)

Ask for any prayer concerns or joys, and invite participants to write these items down in the space provided under next week's Covenant Prayer. This way, the prayer needs will be in front of them as they read throughout the week. Close in a prayer together.

PARTICIPANT GUIDE 2
EPISODE 11—2 Samuel, 1 and 2 Kings
LEADERSHIP
Potential and peril of leadership

More than any other historical period in the Bible, the Israelite monarchy illustrates the double-edged sword of political power: An increased capacity to do good corresponds to a greater potential to do harm. This dynamic has repeated itself throughout human history and is still true about our cultures in the twenty-first century. This episode covers the spectrum of Israelite kings, from the godly to the wicked, to reveal the rewards and consequences of political leadership:

Day 1: David and the height of the empire;
Day 2: Solomon and the division of the kingdom;
Day 3: Ahab and the consequences of ungodliness;
Day 4: Hezekiah and the fall of the northern kingdom; and
Day 5: Josiah and the exile of the southern kingdom.

This episode will help your group:

• analyze what constitutes sound biblical leadership, from the examples of the Israelite kings;
• learn how the role of the prophet offers course-correction to wayward leaders; and
• discover how the promise God made to David is critical to our understanding of covenant theology.

Materials needed: *Covenant Leader Guide*; *Living the Covenant* participant guides; *CEB Study Bible*; *Living the Covenant* DVD (or video download); extra pens or pencils

Optional: An additional video on David and the peril and promise of faithful leadership is available for download from CovenantBibleStudy.com. There is also a video on exile and hope, as well as one retelling the story of Naaman and Elisha.

1. GATHERING TOGETHER (10 min.)

After the Covenant Prayer, invite participants to share examples of people whom they consider to be good leaders. Examples can cover the spectrum from personal to political to cultural. What qualities do their leaders have that makes them good? What makes a leader "good"?

2. REFLECTING TOGETHER (10 min.)

Read together "Our Longing for Relationship" at the beginning of Episode 10 in the participant guide. Invite participants to break up into pairs and share any passages from the week's readings that were particularly meaningful to them. Specifically, have group members explore the question: "How were your interactions with this week's stories shaped by leadership headlines from today's news or from your personal experiences?" Have them share any insights they gained from the questions in the daily readings section of their participant guides. They might also share any verses they chose to memorize for the week.

The life of David plays a central role in how the Israelite monarchy is established and later interpreted. He also illustrates the rewards of faithful leadership and the consequences for making selfish choices. Divide the participants into two groups, and invite each group to compile a list. Have the first group make a list of commendable qualities of David's leadership, including corresponding verses from the readings. Have the second group make a list of the corrupt aspects and negative consequences of David's leadership, along with corresponding verses from the readings. After the groups share their lists, invite them to reflect together on how these two lists often coincide within the same person, as light and shadow, and on how a leader can safely guard against those negative qualities.

In many cases throughout the monarchy, God provides a prophet to serve as a safeguard against corrupt leadership. Have the group divide into as many as five pairs to study the interplay between the king and the divine representative in each of the daily readings:

1. David and Nathan (2 Sam 12)
2. Jeroboam and Ahijah (1 Kgs 11)
3. Ahab and Elijah (1 Kgs 17)
4. Hezekiah and Isaiah (2 Kgs 19)
5. Josiah and the Instruction scroll (2 Kgs 22)

The Instruction scroll isn't a prophet, but it does represent God's corrective action and expectation that were expressed through Moses.

For each reading, have the groups answer these questions: What behaviors of the people or the king warrant correction from God? Was the correction successful? How can a follower of Jesus have a similar prophetic voice against corrupt leadership?

> **Tip:** King or prophet? Think about which form of leadership suits you better and how that shapes the way you function as a leader in this Covenant Bible Study group.

3. VIDEO SEGMENT (25 min.)

The video for Episode 11, on the DVD or available by download, allows the group to overhear a conversation with Roy L. Heller, who is Associate Professor of Old Testament at Perkins School of Theology at Southern Methodist University in Dallas, Texas. Before showing the video, ask the participants to listen for one or more of the following important points:

1. The prophets try to bring royal leaders back to the central notion of relationship, functioning as truth-tellers to Israel's kings. David and the kings who follow him are at their best when they are moved by compassion that draws them out of their preoccupation with power and back to what's best for the people God loves.
2. Nathan tells a story to stir empathy in David and to remind him that relationships, not power, are central to faithful life and leadership.
3. The deepest wisdom of covenant is to love God and love others. Idolatry splits our attention and distorts our priorities, causing us to lose focus on the main thing: God alone is worthy of our absolute loyalty and trust.

At the end of the viewing, choose one of the questions below:

1. How important is compassion in leadership (parenting, teaching, managing employees, holding political office)? Have you ever worked with someone who had a compassion deficit? As an emotional response to another's situation, compassion is more than pity. Compassion takes action. What are some concrete ways to put yourself in another's shoes—and then take action?
2. Why doesn't Nathan simply present David with a good argument against his outrageous behavior? How does a story help the king feel the pain he has caused? How does God appeal to our compassionate core through stories of another's pain? Do you listen for God's call to a changed heart and life in the stories others tell?
3. If idolatry is a kind of distracted loyalty that sends us chasing after every attention-grabbing voice that promises security, what can we do to make God first in our lives? What are some of the forces splintering your attention from the things that are most important to you and to God?

TAKE A BREAK (10 min. optional)

During the break, thank at least one group member for being a prophetic witness to God's love when another member's being right or controlling the conversation distracts group discussion.

4. DISCOVERING TOGETHER (15 min.)

The covenant that God establishes with David in 2 Samuel 7:1-17 is critical to the biblical narrative and to our understanding of covenant. The Group Meeting Experience analyzes various aspects of the covenant with David. Divide the group into two parts, and have the first group answer the first three questions, which are textual analyses of the passage. Have the other group look at the next question, which interprets the role of the covenant in the wider historical and theological context. After both groups share their findings, answer together the last question, which considers the relationship between God's promises and our responsibility.

5. CENTERING TOGETHER (10 min. optional)

It is often difficult to interpret biblical passages without involving our own preconceived assumptions. Both the familiar stories of David and our own political and ideological inclinations about leadership can prevent a fresh hearing of the stories of Samuel and Kings. Lead the group in an experiential reading of 2 Kings 5:1-14 following the guidelines in the Covenant Meditation. Invite the group to share any new qualities they discover that describe a life desired by God.

6. SERVING TOGETHER (5 min.)

Read together the "Signs of Faithful Love" at the end of the episode. Break the participants into pairs, and have them review for a moment any notes they recorded and any insights they gained throughout this episode. Invite them to consider how these stories of Israelite kings might encourage them to become more engaged in leadership, in their families, in the church, and in the wider community.

7. NEXT WEEK (5 min.)

Turn to Episode 12 and briefly introduce next week's title and theme. Encourage participants to select a verse from the readings that they might commit to memory and share next week.

8. CLOSING PRAYER (5 min.)

Ask for any prayer concerns or joys, and invite participants to write these items down in the space provided under next week's Covenant Prayer. This way, the prayer needs will be in front of them as they read throughout the week. Close in a prayer together.

PARTICIPANT GUIDE 2

EPISODE 12—1 and 2 Thessalonians, 1 and 2 Timothy, Titus

GOD'S HOUSEHOLD

To live responsible, changed, and well-ordered lives

Salvation through Jesus Christ is not simply a private affair between individuals and God. God's full plan for redemption also connects people together in community through restored relationships. The Pauline letters of 1 and 2 Thessalonians, 1 and 2 Timothy, and Titus contain many specific instructions to the church regarding how Christians can live in God's household.

This episode will help your group:

- identify the barriers that prevent faithful living;
- determine how to live a life that is pleasing to God; and
- discover how to live in community with each other.

> **Materials needed:** *Covenant Leader Guide*; *Living the Covenant* participant guides; *CEB Study Bible*; *Living the Covenant* DVD (or video download); extra pens or pencils

1. GATHERING TOGETHER (10 min.)

After the Covenant Prayer, invite participants to reflect together on the word *household*. What constitutes a healthy household? What is necessary in order for relationships within the household to be life-giving and mutually beneficial rather than destructive? How does using the image of "household" to describe the church change or challenge our ideas of Christian community?

2. REFLECTING TOGETHER (10 min.)

Read together "Our Longing for Relationship" at the beginning of Episode 12 in the participant guide. Invite participants to break up into pairs and share any passages from the week's readings that were particularly meaningful to them. Specifically, have group members explore the question: "How do these letters from Paul to early Christians seem to be written to you and to your faith community?" Have them share any insights they gained from the questions in the daily readings section of their participant guides. They might also share any verses they chose to memorize for the week.

The letters of 1 and 2 Thessalonians encouraged Christians to maintain their devotion to Jesus Christ in the midst of changing times—in the midst of a culture that was opposed to them. Break the participants into two groups, and have each study the readings for either Day 1 or Day 2. Have them compile two lists based on their texts:

1. threats to faithful living; and
2. how to live a life that pleases God.

For each item on their lists, have them cite the chapter and verse for support. When they are finished, have the groups report their findings to each other. Then ask, "What items on these lists seem most relevant to your life and to the church today?"

The Pastoral Letters of 1 and 2 Timothy and Titus offer specific ways for faithful Christians to live in community with each other. Divide the participants into three groups, and have each group take one of the readings from Days 3, 4, and 5. For each reading, have the groups identify practical guidance that Paul gives for how we can improve our relationships with other Christians and live in harmony with each other. After they have reported their findings to the whole group, ask them to identify which items on their lists seem the most challenging, and which items would make the greatest positive impact if fully realized.

> **Tip:** Good leaders create opportunities for the group to function like a healthy family. Think about sharing a meal and working together to prepare and serve it.

3. VIDEO SEGMENT (25 min.)

The video for Episode 12, on the DVD or available by download, allows the group to overhear a conversation with scholar Audrey L. S. West, a popular Bible teacher in congregations and Adjunct Professor of New Testament at Lutheran School of Theology in Chicago, Illinois. Before showing the video, ask the participants to listen for one of the following important points:

1. First Thessalonians is the earliest letter in the New Testament, written only twenty years after the death and resurrection of Jesus. Paul is writing to a small church whose reputation for love precedes them. He is also trying to encourage a suffering community that he deeply loves. Like letters to those we love today, Paul writes to encourage the church members to hang in there.

2. Second Thessalonians was written much later to a community anxious that Jesus hadn't returned. It was important to Paul that the Thessalonians not get so caught up in anxiety about Jesus' return that they forget how to live with each other.

3. First and Second Timothy record Paul's mentoring relationship with Timothy as a partner in ministry. The first letter is more intimate, while the second reads like a last will and testament. There are challenging aspects to these letters (advice to slaves and masters, for example). The issues must be put in their historical context (for example, advice on clothing and jewelry). They also must be interpreted with knowledge of the specific situations they address and not necessarily as general statements for the church today. Then and now, the most powerful mark and witness of the church is love.

After the video, ask the participants one or two of the questions below:

1. Recall a time when someone cared enough to give you advice worth writing down. Have you ever been a mentor to someone else, offering written advice to keep them on track to live a better life? If you could write a letter to a younger, less-experienced version of yourself, what would you say? What good things about your younger self would you highlight? How would you encourage a younger person to hang in there through suffering?

2. Do you ever let worry about how things will turn out steal your ability to be present to those who need your help right now? What uncertain outcomes have you worrying about the future this week? Stop and pray right now for confidence that God in Jesus Christ will meet your situation at just the right time.

3. Do we adorn ourselves with status symbols today? Is this a problem? How do you decide what advice from the Bible is binding and what advice is specific to the situation of ancient writers and readers? Whom do you trust to help you discern this?

TAKE A BREAK (10 min. optional)

During the break, remind someone in the group of Paul's promise that we will always be with the Lord (see 1 Thess 4:17).

4. DISCOVERING TOGETHER (15 min.)

The Group Meeting Experience takes a closer look at 1 Thessalonians 1:2-10. Focus on who read the letter and on the context of gratitude in which the rest of the letter is grounded. Invite a person in the group to read the text by following the instructions in the first question. Then divide the participants into two groups, each taking two of the four questions. Invite them to explore how the concept of thanksgiving serves as the basis for vital Christian community.

5. CENTERING TOGETHER (10 min. optional)

It's easy to forget that many of the books in the Bible, such as those in this episode, were originally circulated as letters to congregations. Because we have technology that enables private forms of interpersonal communication (e-mail, text messaging, phone calls), it may be difficult to imagine the communal way that these letters were communicated. The Covenant Meditation is a helpful way to experience a text in the way it was first transmitted. If individuals are not doing this during the week, lead the group through the exercise of praying 2 Timothy 3:14-17. Invite the group to share their reflections, encouraging them to interact with the words of scripture as prayers for people within their community.

6. SERVING TOGETHER (5 min.)

Read together the "Signs of Faithful Love" at the end of the episode. Break the participants into pairs, and have them review for a moment any notes they recorded and any insights they gained throughout this episode. Invite them to share how these insights challenge them to find detailed ways to improve specific relationships they have with others in their church communities.

7. NEXT WEEK (5 min.)

Turn to Episode 13 and briefly introduce next week's title and theme. Encourage participants to select a verse from the readings that they might commit to memory and share next week. Be sure to mention that there are additional videos available at CovenantBibleStudy.com for participants who want to enhance their study throughout the week.

8. CLOSING PRAYER (5 min.)

Ask for any prayer concerns or joys, and invite participants to write these items down in the space provided under next week's Covenant Prayer. This way, the prayer needs will be in front of them as they read throughout the week. Close in a prayer together.

PARTICIPANT GUIDE 2

EPISODE 13—Wisdom: Proverbs and Ecclesiastes

DISCERNMENT

Finding what is good for my life

Proverbs and Ecclesiastes suggest that wisdom born from experience is the key to negotiating the complexities and chaos of life. That wisdom is expressed:

Days 1–3: in pithy, portable statements in Proverbs; and

Days 4–5: in the autobiographical prose of Ecclesiastes.

In both cases, the reader is encouraged to engage the world with the task of discernment, for the purpose of determining a life well lived.

This episode will help your group:

- discover crucial insights about proverbs and about how they emerged in schooling for children;
- explore the rich perceptions and skeptical conclusions of Ecclesiastes; and
- learn how to find what is "good" for their personal lives.

> **Materials needed:** *Covenant Leader Guide*; *Living the Covenant* participant guides; *CEB Study Bible*; *Living the Covenant* DVD (or video download); extra pens or pencils
>
> **Optional:** Additional videos on Woman Wisdom (Prov 1) and the wise wife (Prov 31) are available for download from CovenantBibleStudy.com. There is also a video discussing the different kinds of proverbs.

1. GATHERING TOGETHER (10 min.)

After the Covenant Prayer, invite the group to share from their personal experiences the proverbs and sayings they learned as children and that guide their lives. Examples can include statements they often heard repeated by their parents, or phrases they learned in school or read in books. Invite them to reflect on how those statements proved to be true and useful in their lives. What is it about such statements that makes them continually applicable?

2. REFLECTING TOGETHER (10 min.)

Read together "Our Longing for Relationship" at the beginning of the episode. Invite participants to break up into pairs and share any passages from the week's readings that were particularly meaningful to them. Have group members share any insights they gained from the questions in the daily readings section of their participant guides. What particular proverbs or words from Ecclesiastes were helpful to them? They might also share any verses they chose to memorize for the week.

Divide the participants into groups of three, and invite each group to study one of the readings from Days 1–3. Have each person share with others in their group the sayings from their reading that fit each of the following three categories:

1. the proverb that offers the most helpful insight for them;
2. the proverb that seems most contrary to their own wisdom and experience; and
3. the proverb whose lesson is most difficult for them to live out.

After all the persons in each group have shared their opinions, invite each group to look for commonalities among the proverbs selected for each of the three categories. What characterizes the proverbs that are the most helpful? The most contrary? The most challenging?

Now break participants into two groups and invite each group to take one of the readings from Days 4–5. Have the group studying Ecclesiastes 1–4 determine the verses that best resonate with times when their lives have been difficult. Ask the group studying Ecclesiastes 9–12 to determine the verses that offer the best encouragement during trying times. Have each group report their verses to the whole group. Do the conclusions offered at the end of Ecclesiastes resolve the difficulties presented at the beginning? Why or why not? If not, is there any value to what Ecclesiastes offers the person seeking to live a good life?

> **Tip:** You are a voice of wisdom for someone in your Covenant group. Pray for discernment (the ability to read what's good for this person's life), and be ready to respond when they ask for your advice.

3. VIDEO SEGMENT (25 min.)

The video for Episode 13, on the DVD or available by download, allows the group to overhear a conversation with Christine Roy Yoder, who is Professor of Old Testament Language, Literature, and Exegesis at Columbia Theological Seminary in Decatur, Georgia. Before showing the video, ask the participants to listen for one of the following important points:

1. Wisdom literature starts with what is good for human beings and then shows how to navigate life well. Wisdom sayings begin with ordinary, everyday realities and ask not only what is good for individuals, but also what is good for the whole community. With these sayings, the focus shifts from dramatic revelations by God in places like Sinai to everyday life as the setting where wisdom is revealed. Wisdom was drawn from lived experiences among many people across a long period of time. Scribes from the royal court collected these sayings and added their own.

2. Because the sayings are short (easy to learn and remember), wisdom literature names and fits life as it is experienced "on the ground." A moral imagination is required when reading the book of Proverbs. The wise person is one who understands the texts and traditions of faith but can apply them in ways that are life-giving and helpful in real-world circumstances. Knowing the proper time to apply wisdom is the work of discernment, and this involves "putting a moment around the proverb" so it resonates with daily life.

3. Wisdom begins and ends with a healthy fear and humility before the mystery of God. The humble sage or teacher in Ecclesiastes sees a world that doesn't make sense or follow the rules of what's fair or right. The teacher looks for a life-giving word for this world but finds no guarantees: All is vaporous and passing. So Ecclesiastes pulls back from trying to say too much, stressing that life is fragile and short. People should seize the day and enjoy the moments they have now with family and friends, through simple meals and good work done well.

At the end of the viewing, ask one of the questions below:

1. Proverbs are brief sayings built out of life's long experiences. Why do they stick in our memories? What short sayings or proverbs will you pass on to the impressionable young minds in your life?

2. Can you think of someone with a moral imagination—someone who always seems to have the right word at the right time? When the scholar suggests that we "put a moment around a proverb" so it resonates with real life, what does this mean? Think of a situation where what seemed like good advice just didn't fit. Have you ever been on the receiving end of someone's conventional wisdom that failed to fit your circumstances?

3. It's not typical these days to use the language of fear to describe our relationships with God. If there is an inappropriate fear of God (dread of punishment), what does a healthy humility and awe before God look like? Why does this literature suggest that the fear of God is the beginning and ultimate end of wisdom? What are the everyday moments of simple pleasure with family and friends that make life worth living for you? Do you celebrate God in the small things of life? Do you agree with Ecclesiastes that everything in life is pointless or like a puff of air?

TAKE A BREAK (10 min. optional)

During the break, ask someone to listen in the coming weeks for wisdom spoken by other covenant participants and to write these phrases down so they can be shared with the group later. These can be profound, funny, or plainspoken assessments of how things work in the real world.

4. DISCOVERING TOGETHER (15 min.)

The Group Meeting Experience centers on Proverbs 2:1-19, a passage that emphasizes how wisdom is gained through relationships between parents and children and between people and God. Break the participants into two groups. Have the first group answer questions 1–3 and the other group answer questions 4–6. After they have shared their responses, discuss together the final question. How do we search for wisdom today? To what degree is Proverbs 2 a model for that discernment?

5. CENTERING TOGETHER (10 min. optional)

The Covenant Meditation for the week is centered in Ecclesiastes 3:1-8. There is a time for everything under the sun, but the key question to ponder is, "What's good for my life?" This question is posed between opposite poles. Lead the group through the meditation. Invite the group to share their reflections, encouraging them to interact with the words of scripture in a conversation about life lived through these opposites.

6. SERVING TOGETHER (5 min.)

Read together the "Signs of Faithful Love" at the end of the episode. Break the participants into pairs, and have them review for a moment any notes they recorded and any insights they gained throughout this episode. Invite them to share specific ways that they will seek wisdom and live faithfully this week.

7. NEXT WEEK (5 min.)

Turn to Episode 14 and briefly introduce next week's title and theme. Encourage participants to select a verse from the readings that they might commit to memory and share next week.

8. CLOSING PRAYER (5 min.)

Ask for any prayer concerns or joys, and invite participants to write these items down in the space provided under next week's Covenant Prayer. This way, the prayer needs will be in front of them as they read throughout the week. Close in a prayer together.

PARTICIPANT GUIDE 2
EPISODE 14—Philemon, Philippians, Colossians, Ephesians

RECONCILED

Repairing broken relationships

Paul's letters remind us in this week's readings that unity without uniformity has always been a characteristic of the global church. The churches to whom Paul wrote shared common convictions about the saving work of Jesus Christ and about their calling together as the body of Christ. But they each had unique concerns that required individual attention from Paul. Considering both the similarities and the differences among these letters will help us determine what is at the nonnegotiable core of our faith, and what can exist on the fringe with room for disagreement.

This episode will help your group:

- investigate the conflicts in these readings that point to tensions that exist within most faith communities;
- determine what remedies Paul advises to foster reconciliation through Christ; and
- track the continuing evidence of covenant that runs throughout all four letters.

> **Materials needed:** *Covenant Leader Guide*; *Living the Covenant* participant guides; *CEB Study Bible*; *Living the Covenant* DVD (or video download); extra pens or pencils

1. GATHERING TOGETHER (10 min.)

Following the Covenant Prayer, invite participants to reflect on the concepts of unity, uniformity, and diversity when thinking about the church. You may choose to display those three terms and have participants discuss them individually. Use these questions to prompt conversation:

1. Should we expect or strive to be a united global church? (To what degree should different churches be one body of Christ?)

2. To what degree should we expect or strive to be uniform? (What must all churches share in common?)

3. Should we allow ourselves to be, or even strive to be, a diverse church? (How should our faith communities be different from each other?)

2. REFLECTING TOGETHER (10 min.)

Read together "Our Longing for Relationship" at the beginning of Episode 14 in the participant guide. Invite participants to break up into pairs and share any passages from the week's readings that were particularly meaningful to them. Specifically, have group members explore the question: "Did anything that Paul said to these churches seem to describe what is happening in your church?" Have them share any insights they gained from the questions in the daily readings section of their participant guides. They might also share any verses they chose to memorize for the week.

The first two daily readings from Philemon and Philippians contain some vague descriptions of conflict within the church. Paul is seeking reconciliation between Philemon and Onesimus, yet we never fully find out why. Paul is also challenging Euodia and Syntyche in Philippians, yet we never really find out the source of their conflict. Whenever there is a narrative gap in the Bible, it is an invitation for us to fill that gap with what we know about the human condition in our own churches. Divide the participants in half, and have each group take one of the first two daily readings. Have them answer these questions: "What do you think was the source of conflict in these two readings? How does that conflict speak to our human tendency toward conflict in our churches, and how does it relate to any specific conflicts occurring within your church?"

Covenant is a vital theme that runs throughout the entire Bible. In these four letters, we find evidence of people wrestling with the basic questions about being in covenant relationships with God and with each other. Divide participants into four subgroups, and invite each group to read the assigned texts for Ephesians, Philippians, Colossians, and Philemon. For each reading, have them answer these three questions:

1. *Creating the Covenant:* What do these texts tell us about how God creates an opportunity to be in new relationships with us?

2. *Living the Covenant:* What specific guidance does Paul offer the people about how to live a life that is pleasing to God?

3. *Trusting the Covenant:* What barriers exist in these texts that prevent people from being in full relationships with God and from being connected in love with each other?

> **Tip:** Someone in your group is probably experiencing some form of personal captivity to forces beyond their control. Pray that God will give you opportunities to communicate the freedom we share in Jesus Christ with them in a tangible way.

3. VIDEO SEGMENT (25 min.)

The video for Episode 14, on the DVD or available by download, allows the group to overhear a conversation with Michael J. Brown, who is Director of the Malcolm X Institute of Black Studies at Wabash College in Crawfordsville, Indiana. Before showing the video, ask the participants to listen for one of the following conversation points:

1. While imprisoned in chains in a place where hope comes to die, Paul says that God is able to restore hope. These letters reflect that Paul received support during his time in prison. From this place Paul encourages Philemon to be reconciled with Onesimus (a runaway slave) because both are "in Christ."
2. In Philippians, Paul passes on an early hymn, speaking of the complete self-emptying of Jesus as the servant who suffers for our sins and who is exalted by God.
3. Paul is not a systematic theologian, but instead a pastoral thinker dealing with real congregations. His words about slaves and masters must be understood in his context, where the return of Jesus was expected soon.

At the end of the viewing, ask one of the questions below:

1. Jesus said, "I was in prison and you visited me" (Matt 25:36). Have you or someone you know served time in prison? Have you ever visited a jail or prison? How do the people in your neighborhood or social circles feel about convicted criminals? How does Paul's situation or that of Onesimus help us think about the deeper meaning of reconciliation? Does Israel's central story connect with the suffering of those held captive or on the run after being set free? How?
2. Is self-sacrifice a Christian value to be imitated? Can you think of ways this ideal has been abused or forced on those with less power? Is it significant that Jesus emptied himself (and therefore wasn't forced to serve)? Why? What would self-emptying look like in a healthy life today?
3. How do you read Paul's advice to slaves and masters? How does belonging to each other "in Christ" change the rules for our relationships? Who could say to you, "I won't mention that you owe me your life" (Phlm 1:19)?

TAKE A BREAK (10 min. optional)

During the break, think about persons in the group who need reconciliation in their lives and about what you can do to help them experience freedom in Christ.

4. DISCOVERING TOGETHER (15 min.)

Though conflict is inevitable in any human community, Paul offers the churches in this week's readings clear guidance on how to resolve differences and be reconciled with each other. The Group Meeting Experience takes a closer look at how Christians can be restored in their relationships with each other. Invite a person to read aloud Ephesians 2:1-22, and divide the participants into five groups to answer the five questions. Afterward, invite participants to share specific ways that Paul's guidance can be applied to conflict situations in their own church.

5. CENTERING TOGETHER (10 min. optional)

A deeply personal and intimately written letter like the one Paul wrote to Philemon is conducive to spiritual reading. The Covenant Meditation invites participants to read the four verses of Philemon 4-7 as a prayer, evoking images of actual people with whom they might need to be reconciled. Lead the group in this exercise, and allow time for them to reflect with each other on ways they feel led to reconnect with people in their lives with whom they are in conflict.

6. SERVING TOGETHER (5 min.)

Read together the "Signs of Faithful Love" at the end of the episode. Break the participants into pairs, and have them review for a moment any notes they recorded and any insights they gained throughout this episode. Invite them to share how these insights challenge them to find detailed ways to seek reconciliation among disconnected people in their faith community.

7. NEXT WEEK (5 min.)

Turn to Episode 15 and briefly introduce next week's title and theme. Encourage participants to select a verse from the readings that they might commit to memory and share next week. Be sure to mention that there are additional videos available at CovenantBibleStudy.com for participants who want to enhance their study throughout the week.

8. CLOSING PRAYER (5 min.)

Ask for any prayer concerns or joys, and invite participants to write these items down in the space provided under next week's Covenant Prayer. This way, the prayer needs will be in front of them as they read throughout the week. Close in a prayer together.

PARTICIPANT GUIDE 2

EPISODE 15—James, Jude, 1 and 2 Peter

ACT LIKE A CHRISTIAN

Practicing what we believe

Pursuing the Christian life brings tensions between the lives we are to live and the pressures that prevent us from doing so. Those threats include:

Days 1–2: the standards of the world;
Day 3: our old selfish desires;
Day 4: harassment from others; and
Day 5: ambiguity about eternity.

Each of this week's readings contains practical responses to these pressures and guides Christians toward living lives that are pleasing to God.

This episode will help your group:

- identify the practical guidance offered by these books to alter their behavior;
- investigate the tensions that exist in living the Christian life; and
- discover the Old Testament roots that inform 1 Peter and discover their relevance to Christian faith and living.

> **Materials needed:** *Covenant Leader Guide*; *Living the Covenant* participant guides; *CEB Study Bible*; *Living the Covenant* DVD (or video download); extra pens or pencils
>
> **Optional:** An additional video on James and Paul is available for download from CovenantBibleStudy.com, as well as a video on how the book of James speaks about the tongue.

1. GATHERING TOGETHER (10 min.)

The readings from this week highlight the perilous power of words ("the tongue" in Jas 3). Following the Covenant Prayer, invite participants to reflect together on a time when they (or someone they know) sent an e-mail or a text, or spoke a harmful word that hurt someone else or damaged a relationship. Have them also consider a time when someone (a teacher, a friend, a family member, or a coworker) spoke a blessing into their lives, saying just the right thing at just the right time. Can harmful words be taken back? Why or why not? What spoken or written words do the participants wish they could take back?

> **Tip:** James says the tongue is a rudder that steers the ship and a flame that sets the world on fire (Jas 3:1-6). The context refers to the perils of being a teacher or a leader! Ask God to let the words that come out of your mouth build up and encourage rather than shipwreck and set ablaze (Ps 19:14).

2. REFLECTING TOGETHER (10 min.)

Read together "Our Longing for Relationship" at the beginning of Episode 15 in the participant guide. Invite participants to break up into pairs and share any passages from the week's readings that were particularly meaningful to them. Specifically, have group members explore the question: "What did you discover from these readings about how to live a faithful Christian life?" Have them share any insights they gained from the questions in the daily readings section of their participant guides. They might also share any verses they chose to memorize for the week.

The book of James contains a great amount of practical advice for how Christians should behave. Invite the group to discuss the relationship between faith and works. What is the role of good works in the Christian life? If there is nothing we can do to be saved, what does the letter from James mean when it says, "Faith without actions has no value at all" (Jas 2:20)? Next, divide the participants into five groups and invite them each to take a chapter of James. Have the participants in each group make a list of everything in their chapter that James advocates for how to live a holy life. What behaviors are difficult to perform, and what makes them difficult?

The books of 1 and 2 Peter and Jude confront some of the inherent challenges to living as "immigrants" and "strangers" in the world today. Divide the participants into three groups, and have each group take a closer look at either 1 Peter, 2 Peter, or Jude. Have them identify what their book claims is a primary difficulty or obstacle that prevents Christians from living a righteous life. Then ask them to answer the question: "What good news does this book offer us that would encourage us to live faithful lives?" Allow time for the groups to share their discoveries with each other.

3. VIDEO SEGMENT (25 min.)

The video for Episode 15, on the DVD or available by download, allows the group to overhear a conversation with David L. Bartlett, who is Professor Emeritus of Christian Communication at Yale Divinity School. Before showing the video, ask the participants to listen for one of the following important points:

1. James, Jude, and 1 and 2 Peter are written to churches suffering harassment and struggling to keep faith when Jesus' expected return hasn't happened. The authors wanted the readers of these circulating letters that were dispersed throughout the empire to stay tied to the tradition of faith, so they wrote in the names of those key followers close to Jesus and the early church. The authors found a way to make the tradition speak to new circumstances and to a new situation.

2. James is a practical letter, deeply steeped in who God is and what God is doing. By presenting the depth of God's intentions and what you should do about those intentions, James is particularly concerned about gossip in the church and favoritism toward the rich. Though he doesn't mention Christ very often, James is a splendid example of the embodiment of the Christlike life.

3. First Peter is written to seven churches, which have come to symbolize the universal church and what it was going through in his time. The immigrant and dispersed church is called to negotiate faithfulness by navigating the culture and adapting where possible. Because Jesus isn't coming as soon as we thought, we must find ways to negotiate life in a world with its own values and pictures of what our relationships should look like (submission, slavery, male dominance, and so on). Discernment is required to recognize the things in our faith that are nonnegotiable (trust in Christ, courage, not practicing idolatry, and so on).

After the video, ask group members one of the questions below:

1. The situation of the believers originally addressed by these books is one of "negotiated faithfulness." Have you ever found yourself in an environment (or even another country or culture) with a surprisingly different set of values than yours? What happened? How did you navigate this culture clash? What were your "nonnegotiables"?

2. James says God doesn't play favorites and is unimpressed by privilege and power. Think of a situation where you were shown favoritism. When have you seen people who are poor treated differently from the affluent? Why do you think this bothers James (and God) so much? If wealth doesn't measure our value in God's eyes, what does?

3. Relationships were defined by different values and boundaries in the ancient world than those that make sense to us today. Is the marriage model of submission in the Greco-Roman household as rich an image as the mutual love of Christ and the church from the letter to the Ephesians?

TAKE A BREAK (10 min. optional)

During the break, ask group members if they are having any trouble keeping up with the reading. Confess your own struggles to keep up and ask what would help (audio Bible? e-mail reminders?).

4. DISCOVERING TOGETHER (15 min.)

The Group Meeting Experience investigates the Old Testament foundations of 1 Peter 2:4-10. Ask for seven volunteers to look up and read aloud the passages listed in the first question. Then divide the participants into three groups and ask each one to answer questions 2–4. After all the groups have shared their conclusions, discuss the last question together. What connections can the group make between this passage and the church today?

5. CENTERING TOGETHER (10 min. optional)

The passage for this week's Covenant Meditation, James 1:22-26, clearly challenges us to put our convictions into action. Lead the group in the exercise as instructed by the meditation, inviting participants to be open to specific areas of their lives that need to be surrendered to God. Following the activity, invite them to share with a partner any insights they gained from the text and the specific ways they will put those insights into practice.

6. SERVING TOGETHER (5 min.)

Read together the "Signs of Faithful Love" at the end of the episode. Break the participants into pairs, and have them review for a moment any notes they recorded and any insights they gained throughout this episode. Invite them to share how these insights will translate into tangible changes in their behavior this week.

7. NEXT WEEK (5 min.)

Turn to Episode 16 and briefly introduce next week's title and theme. Encourage participants to select a verse from the readings that they might commit to memory and share next week.

Encourage the participants to stay committed to their Covenant group relationships after the second milestone is reached with Episode 16. If you decide to take a break for a week or more after Episode 16, discuss with the group the date when you will start back up with the next participant guide: *Trusting the Covenant*. Be sure to update your group calendar at CovenantBibleStudy.com if you take a break. This third segment is especially beneficial to participants because they will learn how to trust their relationships when times are troubled.

8. CLOSING PRAYER (5 min.)

Ask for any prayer concerns or joys, and invite participants to write these items down in the space provided under next week's Covenant Prayer. This way, the prayer needs will be in front of them as they read throughout the week. Close in a prayer together.

PARTICIPANT GUIDE 2

EPISODE 16—Prophets: Isaiah 1-39 and the Book of the Twelve

Doing the Right Thing

What should we do?

With destruction about to happen all around them, the Israelites faced some tough questions about the results of their own rebellion. Their suffering became a clear reminder that sin often has consequences. Yet, even in the midst of their ruin, God hadn't abandoned them. The prophets offered a corrective voice to challenge them in the way of righteousness and social justice, and even provided a word of hope for the depressed survivors. This week's readings explore Isaiah 1–39 (Day 1), the most prolific of the Hebrew prophets, along with a sampling of other prophets that are part of the Book of the Twelve (or Minor Prophets): Hosea (Day 2); Amos (Day 3); Micah (Day 4); and Zephaniah (Day 5).

This week's episode, which is a transition toward the third participant guide, titled *Trusting the Covenant*, will help your group:

- gain a deeper understanding of how each prophet diagnoses the sinful condition of God's people;
- discover the unique way that each prophet calls the people to seek justice; and
- perceive and sense hope from the prophets, which can apply to trying times.

Materials needed: *Covenant Leader Guide*; *Living the Covenant* participant guides; *CEB Study Bible*; *Living the Covenant* DVD (or video download); extra pens or pencils

Optional: An additional video on defining a prophet is available for download from CovenantBibleStudy.com, as well as a video on Isaiah and Amos.

COVENANTLeader Guide

1. GATHERING TOGETHER (10 min.)

Remind participants that our use of the word *prophet* doesn't indicate "one who foretells the future." While a prophet often sharpened a keen political sense about what was coming toward God's people, a biblical prophet was one who gave a corrective, challenging, and hopeful word from God to people who had lost their way. Pray the Covenant Prayer and invite participants to reflect on particular people in their lives who have served such a role for them. Ask them: "Who are the people who have been prophetic voices to you? What were the encouraging or challenging messages they shared with you, and what difference did they prompt in your lives?"

2. REFLECTING TOGETHER (10 min.)

Read together the "Our Longing for Relationship" at the beginning of Episode 16 in the participant guide. Invite participants to break up into pairs and share any passages from the week's readings that were particularly meaningful to them. Specifically, have group members explore the question: "What words, phrases, or images were significant or memorable to you this week, and why?" Have them share any insights they gained from the questions in the daily readings section of their participant guides. They might also share any verses they chose to memorize for the week.

Divide the participants into as many as five groups, inviting each group to explore one of the daily readings:

1. Have each group identify how the prophet in their reading describes the rebellion of the Israelites: What was their sin? What was the consequence? Is there any person or group of people today living in a similarly wayward fashion?
2. Have them identify the verses that describe how the prophet calls people to seek justice, equality, personal responsibility, or concern for others. How does that call for justice rectify their sinful choices? And how might carrying out that call for justice today make a difference in the world?
3. Have them identify the verses that show how the prophet offers hope for the future. What does God promise to the people? Is that promise conditional—that is, based on the people's returning to faithful living? How might that be a hopeful word for today?

After all the groups have shared their findings with each other, ask them to discuss together what these discoveries reveal about "the pathos of God" described in the workbook. Are we to be troubled by a God who gets angry and emotional? Is there anything hopeful or redemptive about being in a relationship with a God who is affected by our actions, rather than one who is cold and distant?

> **Tip:** Find a video link online with a brief speech by a prophetic voice from our time. Note the feelings you have when you listen to this person's voice: fear, excitement, anger, sympathy, longing, or hope. Keep this feeling response in mind as you lead your group's discussion of the prophets.

3. VIDEO SEGMENT (25 min.)

The video for Episode 16, on the DVD or available by download, allows the group to overhear a conversation with Francisco García-Treto, who is Professor Emeritus of Religion at Trinity University in San Antonio, Texas. Before showing the video, ask the participants to listen for one of the following important points:

1. Through their messages and actions, the prophets express the feelings of God: God's deep love for Israel and all of humanity, and God's deep pain, disappointment, and anger when they don't act like the human beings they were made to be.
2. The prophets want the people to remember what it means to be a loving community of neighbors. They communicate God's yearning to call the people back to taking care of each other—especially those they are most likely to exclude (widows, orphans, strangers/immigrants) in the pursuit of privilege and entitlement.
3. The prophets (for example, Hosea) also express God's parental heart and God's refusal to give up on a faithless people.

After the video, ask group members one or two of the following questions:

1. Think of a time when someone you know deeply disappointed or angered their parents. What were the consequences? Was their parents' anger justified? What actions did either parent take to restore the relationship?
2. The prophets measure the covenant community's faithfulness by their treatment of the most vulnerable people in their midst. Do you think it actually breaks God's heart when we forget people on the margins of society? Why is this so important to God?
3. Christine Chakoian told the story of the power of prayer expressed in "pray-ins" or "kneel-ins" on the steps of churches during the civil rights movement. Are there actions that people of faith can take today to express both our love for God and God's heartbrokenness and disappointment in the way we treat each other? Think of some examples.

TAKE A BREAK (10 min. optional)

During the break, ask someone in the group if their family welcomed prophetic voices (Gandhi, Dr. Martin Luther King, Jr., and so on) in the past or saw them as troublemakers.

4. DISCOVERING TOGETHER (15 min.)

The Group Meeting Experience takes a closer look at Amos 5:7-24, which offers a sharp diagnosis of the people's unfaithfulness and encourages them to seek justice and righteousness. Have someone read aloud the text, then break the group into small subgroups of two or three and have them answer the questions in the participant guide. Be sure to allow enough time for them to share their conclusions, and invite the whole class to reflect together on the final question: Who are today's prophets?

5. CENTERING TOGETHER (10 min. optional)

The passage for this week's meditation, Micah 6:8, is an excellent brief mission statement for God's covenant people: "to do justice, embrace faithful love, and walk humbly with your God." Lead the group in the exercise as instructed by the Covenant Meditation, inviting participants to be open to specific areas of their lives that could change the world with God's justice. Following the meditation, invite group members to share with a partner any insights they gained from the text and the specific ways they will put those insights into practice.

6. SERVING TOGETHER (5 min.)

Read together the "Signs of Faithful Love" at the end of the episode. Break the participants into pairs, and have them review for a moment any notes they recorded and any insights they gained throughout this episode. Invite them to consider how they are specifically challenged to listen to the voices of prophets today and to seek justice and righteousness in the world.

7. NEXT EIGHT WEEKS: *TRUSTING THE COVENANT* (5 min.)

Turn to Episode 17 in the *Trusting the Covenant* participant guide, and briefly introduce the title and theme. Encourage participants to select a verse from the readings that they might commit to memory and share when you next meet. Also mention that there are additional videos available at CovenantBibleStudy.com for participants who want to enhance their study of John's writings.

Celebrate the completion of the first sixteen episodes. Encourage the participants to stay committed to their Covenant group relationships now that the second milestone has been reached with Episode 16. If you decide to take a break for a week or more after Episode 16, discuss with the group the date when you will start back up with the next participant guide: *Trusting the Covenant*. Remember to update your group calendar at CovenantBibleStudy.com so that daily scripture readings are e-mailed at the right times.

8. CLOSING PRAYER (5 min.)

Ask for any prayer concerns or joys, and invite participants to write these items down in the space provided under next week's Covenant Prayer (Episode 17 in the *Trusting the Covenant* participant guide). This way, the prayer needs will be in front of them as they read throughout the week. Close in a prayer together.

PARTICIPANT GUIDE 3
EPISODE 17—John; 1, 2, and 3 John
LIFE TOGETHER
Abundant, eternal life with others

John's Gospel and John's letters offer a framework for mature Christian beliefs and behaviors. The good news demonstrates how a Christian community is to live well together, even under stress and during dangerous times (especially by 100 CE, some seventy years after Jesus' resurrection). In John, Jesus encounters many kinds of people (for example, Nicodemus and the Samaritan woman), and he performs signs that bridge our differences into common identity and purpose. The daily readings from this week highlight how the dearly loved community should be formed:

Day 1: as people of the light;
Day 2: as healed disciples;
Day 3: through an intimate connection to Jesus;
Day 4: by resurrection; and most importantly,
Day 5: through love of God and of each other.

This episode will help your group:

- become familiar with John's use of imagery in his account of Jesus;
- encounter unique people in John's Gospel who embody a healthy response to Jesus; and
- discover the identity and the purpose of Jesus' dearly loved community.

Materials needed: *Covenant Leader Guide*; *Trusting the Covenant* participant guides; *CEB Study Bible*; *Trusting the Covenant* DVD (or video download); extra pens or pencils

Optional: An additional video on incarnation and abundant love is available for download from CovenantBibleStudy.com. There are also three other videos retelling the stories of Nicodemus, Mary Magdalene at the tomb, and Jesus and the Samaritan woman at the well.

1. GATHERING TOGETHER (10 min.)

After praying the Covenant Prayer, invite participants to consider how shared imagery defines many communities today. After an opening prayer, divide participants into groups of two or three, and invite them to reflect on this question: "What examples can you give, either personally or culturally, of people groups who are shaped by common symbols?"

Examples might be visual (a family coat of arms, a denominational logo, a national flag) or verbal (a family saying; the motto of an alma mater; a cultural idiom [for example, the "Volunteer State"]; or a corporate slogan). How do these symbols carry great meaning in defining the ideals and purpose of a community?

> **Tip:** In theater and film, a "character secret" often motivates an actor's performance. This secret is something about the character that no one except the actor knows that explains why that character feels and acts the way they do. Is there a story in the Gospel of John that resonates with your own experience of Jesus as God with us? Without sharing it with the group, let this be your own character secret as a leader, shaping your interaction with the group during your conversation about the Gospel of John.

2. REFLECTING TOGETHER (10 min.)

Read together "Our Longing for Relationship" at the beginning of Episode 17 in the third participant guide. Invite participants to break up into pairs and share any passages from the week's readings that were particularly meaningful to them. Have group members share any insights they gained about John's Gospel and letters from the questions in the daily readings section of their participant guides. They might also share any verses they chose to memorize for the week.

Divide the participants into small groups of two or three, and have each subgroup explore further one of five characters (or groups of characters) that John shares either exclusively or uniquely in his Gospel: Nicodemus (John 3:1-21); the Samaritan woman (John 4:4-42); the blind man (John 9:1-38); Lazarus, Mary, and Martha (John 11:1-46); and Pilate (John 18:28–19:16a). For each of these characters, have group members answer the following questions:

1. What choices does this character face in response to the words and actions of Jesus?
2. Why are these choices difficult for this character?
3. What are the positive and negative consequences of the choices this character makes?

After all the subgroups have reported to the whole group, discuss how these choices might constitute John's ideal definition of the faithful community.

Next, divide the participants into two subgroups, and have one group look at the reading for Day 3 (John 14–17) and the other group look at the reading for Day 5 (1 John 2–4; 2 John; and 3 John). For those looking at John 14–17, invite them to come up with a list of adjectives that would describe the community of believers according to John. Invite those reading John's letters to come up with a list of verbs that would describe the mission and purpose of the community of believers. After both groups have reported, discuss how close your own congregation is to embodying the qualities of both lists.

3. VIDEO SEGMENT (25 min.)

The video for Episode 17, on the DVD or available by download, gives the group a chance to overhear a conversation with Jaime Clark-Soles, who is Associate Professor of New Testament at Perkins School of Theology at Southern Methodist University in Dallas, Texas. Before showing the video, ask the participants to listen for the following key conversation points:

1. God in Jesus is the one who keeps coming into the world, always reaching out to us and going out of the way to be in relationship with us.
2. Jesus meets his followers in whatever ways they need with new life, drawing them back into the community.
3. We have access to the same Someone to get us through tough times that Jesus promised to all who follow him: the Holy Spirit.

At the end of the viewing, choose one or two of the following questions to ask:

1. How does the "looking-for-us-first" God fit with the picture of God's faithful love in the Old Testament? What does this mean for those of us who are more (or less) inclined to be "seekers"? Where would Jesus find you if he were seeking you out this week?
2. John is a very relational Gospel with "room to spare" in God's household and at God's table. Can you think of people who some might feel uncomfortable welcoming into God's "room-to-spare" household? What are some practical ways we can share God's welcome with people in everyday life (at work, school, on the streets where we live)?
3. Has the risen Jesus drawn you (or someone you know) back into the community of followers? What happened?

TAKE A BREAK (10 min. optional)

During the break, ask someone to share their favorite "I am" saying of Jesus: living bread (John 6:51); light of the world (John 9:5); the gate of the sheep (John 10:7); the good shepherd (John 10:11); the resurrection and the life (John 11:25); the way, the truth, and the life (John 14:6); or the true vine (John 15:1).

4. DISCOVERING TOGETHER (15 min.)

Invite someone in the group to read aloud John 12:1-6, and have someone else read aloud John 13:1-17. Invite the group to reflect together on the power of human touch evident in both stories. Ask them to discuss how touch creates intimacy and deep connection between people, and what these two stories might suggest about the relationships between believers and each other and with Jesus.

Divide the group into pairs and invite them to work from their participant guides through the three questions in the Group Meeting Experience together. Allow time for the pairs to share their findings with the full group.

5. CENTERING TOGETHER (10 min. optional)

John's Gospel is a visual book. It's loaded with visual and verbal images that define the ideals of the faith community. Therefore, it is best experienced visually, drawing together the meaning that individuals elicit from an image as a way of forming common bonds. Lead the group in an experience of meditating on scripture by following the instructions for the Covenant Meditation on John 15:9-13 in their participant guides. Be sure to allow time for participants to share with others what words or phrases are meaningful to them.

6. SERVING TOGETHER (5 min.)

Read together the "Signs of Faithful Love" at the end of the episode. Break the participants into pairs, and have them review for a moment any notes they recorded and any insights they gained throughout this episode. Invite them to consider how John's Gospel and John's letters might shape the identity and mission of their congregation. Ask, "What tangible actions are you challenged to undertake as a result of this week's experience?" (for example: visiting a lonely person who has too little physical contact). By now in the Covenant Bible Study, the group may be thinking together about a service project to meet a need in their community. Visit CovenantBibleStudy.com for some service ideas.

7. NEXT WEEK (5 min.)

Turn to Episode 18 and briefly introduce next week's title and theme. Encourage participants to select a verse from the readings that they might commit to memory and share next week. Also mention that there are additional videos available at CovenantBibleStudy.com for participants who want to enhance their study throughout the week. Invite them to bring an MP3 player, smart phone, or other mobile device with music they like to listen to when they are happy, resting, worshipping, or exercising (see the "Gathering Together" section in Episode 18 of the leader guide).

8. CLOSING PRAYER (5 min.)

Ask for any prayer concerns or joys, and invite participants to write these items down in the space provided under next week's Covenant Prayer. This way, the prayer needs will be in front of them as they read throughout the week. Close in a prayer together.

PARTICIPANT GUIDE 3
EPISODE 18—Psalms
PRAISE AND LAMENT
Bring everything to God in prayer.

More than any other book in the Bible, the Psalms give language to life's most solemn and joyous moments. They cover the entire gamut of human experience and the diversity of human emotions. More importantly, psalms teach us how to communicate in prayer as we develop a faithful relationship with God. The readings for this episode point to five key purposes for the disciplined practice of communicating with God in prayer:

Day 1: obedience;
Day 2: lament;
Day 3: gratitude;
Day 4: humility; and
Day 5: praise.

Keeping these five purposes in balance through prayer is vital to mature discipleship.

This episode will help your group:

- become familiar with the basic types and parts of the Psalms;
- discover how the images and concerns contained in the Psalms can express their yearnings, desires, and anxieties on any given day; and
- learn how to more fully incorporate the Psalms into their personal devotional lives.

Materials needed: *Covenant Leader Guide*; *Trusting the Covenant* participant guides; *CEB Study Bible*; *Trusting the Covenant* DVD (or video download); extra pens or pencils; songs for the "Gathering Together" exercise (on personal MP3 players)

Optional: An additional video on the Psalms—which we speak aloud in worship and which tell our contemporary stories—is available for download from CovenantBibleStudy.com.

1. GATHERING TOGETHER (10 min.)

Invite participants in advance to bring their personal MP3 players (for example, an iPod, a tablet, or a phone). After the Covenant Prayer, divide participants into pairs and invite them to share with each other the titles (or even play a few seconds) of songs they prefer to listen to when experiencing these different life situations:

- joy and celebration;
- quiet rest;
- physical exercise;
- grief or sadness; and
- worship and inspiration.

Why is it important to have a full emotional range of music at our ready disposal throughout life? Ask group members to reflect on the differences between hearing or singing the music on the one hand and simply reading the lyrics on the other. What is gained or lost by just reading the words? (If you encounter a participant who claims to have no recorded music in their life, suggest that the group member identify a favorite psalm or hymn that expresses their desires or concerns.)

> **Tip:** Bring your own song, and lead with a short selection from it. Listen to short portions of as many songs as time permits. If a participant took time to bring a song, they will probably have a deep connection to the music, so encourage the group to respect every genre no matter how different it might be from their own individual tastes.

2. REFLECTING TOGETHER (10 min.)

Read together "Our Longing for Relationship" at the beginning of Episode 18 in the participant guide. Invite participants to break up into pairs and share any passages from the week's readings that were particularly meaningful to them. Have group members share any insights they gained about the Psalms from the questions in the daily readings section of their participant guides. They might also share any verses they chose to memorize for the week.

Divide the participants into smaller groups of two or three, and have each group analyze one set of the daily readings. Ask them to describe the personal scenarios in which someone might find it helpful to read their particular set of psalms. (For example, "A person might read Psalm 1 when feeling pressured by others to take a cheap shortcut in life.") Then ask them to discern what that psalm reveals about (1) the character of God; and (2) the benefits of living out the words of that psalm. (Some biblical words or phrases that define God's character include *patience*, *loyal love*, *forgiving*, *angry*, *creative*, *knowing*, *examining*, *healing*, *expectant*, *present*, *nearby*, *far above*, and many more.)

Several of the readings suggest a "before and after" picture of one who experiences God's faithful love. Keeping the same subgroups, have each group read one of the following psalms: 1; 13; 22; 90; or 107. Then have them identify the key moment in the psalm where the mood changes from negative to positive. What characterizes humanity before and after God intervenes? What prescriptions do these psalms give to those in distress?

3. VIDEO SEGMENT (25 min.)

The video for Episode 18, on the DVD or available by download, gives the group a chance to overhear a conversation with William P. Brown, who is Professor of Old Testament at Columbia Theological Seminary in Decatur, Georgia. Before showing the video, ask the participants to listen for one of the following key conversation points:

1. The Psalms are songs, poems, and prayers to and about God with three major types or genres: laments, thanksgiving, and praise (or, as one writer says, "help, thanks, and wow").
2. While God wears many faces in the Psalms, and while there is a diversity of authorship across the 150 chapters, the Psalms are user-friendly and give voice to our conflicts, our confessions, and especially our cries for God's rescuing and saving help (stand up, wake up, help me, God).
3. The Psalms teach us how to pray with the courage to express complaints to God, trusting that God's primary character trait of faithful love will mean deliverance and salvation.

After viewing the video, choose one or two of these questions to ask:

1. Is there a "sound track" to key moments (good times and bad) in your life? Do you have a tune that was "our song," or do you remember a summer pop song from your youth? What about campfire songs, breakup songs, senior year songs, or something sung at your wedding, in the shower, or at the top of your lungs alone with the car windows rolled up?
2. Think of songs we sing together (the national anthem at a ballgame, happy birthday, the doxology). Do you prefer solos or sing-alongs? Why?
3. Why do you think so many psalms switch from cries of despair for help (laments) to songs of praise and thanksgiving? Does that pattern follow in your own life?

TAKE A BREAK (10 min. optional)

During the break, ask if anyone remembers the "rate-a-record" segment from *American Bandstand*. What were some of the teens' responses that group members can recall (it has a good beat, you can dance to it, and so on)?

4. DISCOVERING TOGETHER (15 min.)

Have participants turn to the Group Meeting Experience in their participant guides. Discuss the first question together, then invite them to think of other places in the Psalms that the image of water plays an important role; for example, Psalm 1, in which the one who follows God's Instruction (Torah) is like a tree replanted by streams of water. Ask them to think of other biblical stories in which water is significant. Why is this an important metaphor throughout the Bible? (Observe that the Bible begins with God hovering over the water as creation begins in Genesis 1, and it ends with "the river of life-giving water" in Revelation 22.) How does the significance of water inform our understanding of baptism?

Divide the group into pairs, and invite the pairs to work through the remaining three questions together. As time permits, allow the pairs to share their findings with the full group.

5. CENTERING TOGETHER (10 min. optional)

Psalms is a liturgical book, which means that it is best experienced in the context of a worshipping community when directing prayerful attention to God. Lead the group in an experience of the Covenant Meditation on Psalm 139:1-6 in the participant guide. Following the exercise, invite them to share with a partner what word or phrase came to mind. Then ask them to consider how they might incorporate this way of using the Psalms into their daily lives. What barriers might prevent them from praying through the Psalms in this way, and how can those barriers be overcome?

6. SERVING TOGETHER (5 min.)

Read together the "Signs of Faithful Love" at the end of the episode. Break the participants into pairs, and have them review for a moment any notes they recorded and any insights they gained throughout this episode. Invite them to consider how they might use the Psalms more intentionally in their personal devotional life. How might the Psalms direct them to deepen their relationships with God? How might the Psalms guide them to serve others and share God's love with the world? Have group members share with each other how the Psalms will shape their behavior in the coming week.

7. NEXT WEEK (5 min.)

Turn to Episode 19 and briefly introduce next week's title and theme. Encourage participants to select a verse from the readings that they might commit to memory and share next week.

8. CLOSING PRAYER (5 min.)

Ask for any prayer concerns or joys, and invite participants to write these items down in the space provided under next week's Covenant Prayer. This way, the prayer needs will be in front of them as they read throughout the week. Close in a prayer together.

PARTICIPANT GUIDE 3
EPISODE 19—Job
TRAGEDY
God's role in human suffering

Suffering is a common part of life. It helps to define us as human beings. Jesus also experienced suffering. Even if we aren't suffering personally at the moment, we are relating to someone who is. So whether we can identify with Job or his friends, we have many entry points into this book. Job is a knotty book, introducing a complex range of responses to the nature of suffering, including readings for:

Day 1: the traditional response;
Day 2: the anguished response; and
Day 3: the well-meaning but unhelpful response.

The most complicated parts of the book come from readings on:

Day 4: God's response; and
Day 5: the conclusion to the story.

This episode will help your group:

- discover the complex theological responses to suffering presented by the book of Job and weigh the pros and cons of each one;
- utilize the Covenant Meditation to develop empathy for those who are suffering; and
- determine practical ways to alleviate the suffering of others.

Materials needed: *Covenant Leader Guide*; *Trusting the Covenant* participant guides; *CEB Study Bible*; *Trusting the Covenant* DVD (or video download); extra pens or pencils

1. GATHERING TOGETHER (10 min.)

A theodicy (*theo* = God; and *dicy* = justice) is an attempt to solve the problem of pain by examining God's justice. After the Covenant Prayer, invite participants to consider how they have personally wrestled with the problem of pain, which can be stated as follows: "If God is all-loving and all-powerful, why is there suffering in the world?" Invite participants to share from personal experiences and contemporary events without having the group come to any clear theological conclusions yet.

> **Tip:** Listen carefully for any personal stories of pain, tragedy, and disappointment with God underlying this discussion (shared or private). If you have your own story of loss or devastation, allow the memory and feelings associated with it to inform how you lead this discussion.

2. REFLECTING TOGETHER (10 min.)

Read together "Our Longing for Relationship" at the beginning of Episode 19 in the participant guide. Invite participants to break up into pairs and share any passages from the week's readings that were particularly meaningful to them. Specifically, have group members explore the question: "How did your personal experiences of suffering and tragedy shape your interaction with the readings from Job?" Have them share any insights they gained from the questions in the daily readings section of their participant guides. They might also share any verses they chose to memorize for the week.

Divide the group into smaller groups, and have each subgroup explore one way that the book of Job explains the reasons for human suffering:

1. Suffering is God's way of testing us (Job 2:10).
2. Suffering is part of God's will and plan (Job 9:22-24; 19:8-12).
3. Suffering makes us stronger (Job 5:17-27).
4. Suffering corrects our waywardness (Job 8:1-7).
5. Suffering reminds us that God's ways are a mystery (Job 11:5-12).

For each type of reason, have the groups answer these questions: "What is sensible or acceptable about this reason for suffering? What is difficult to understand or accept about this reason for suffering?"

Next, divide the group into two subgroups, and have one group study God's response to Job in the reading for Day 4 (Job 38–41). Have them answer the questions: "What do you think is the reason for God to respond to Job in this way? Is God being a bully? Is God trying to change the subject and divert Job's attention to the grandeur of creation? Or is God trying to teach Job an important lesson? If so, what is that lesson?"

Have the other group explore Job's response in the reading for Day 5 (Job 42:1-17, particularly 42:6). What is the motivation behind Job's response to God? Is it satisfaction with God's response? Is it sarcasm? Is it exhausted resignation? After both groups report their conclusions, discuss what they think about God's role in suffering.

3. VIDEO SEGMENT (25 min.)

The video for Episode 19, on the DVD or available by download, allows the group to overhear a conversation with Amy Erickson, who is Assistant Professor of Hebrew Bible at Iliff School of Theology in Denver, Colorado. Before showing the video, ask the participants to listen for some of the following important points:

1. The book of Job is staging several difficult human questions: Why do human beings worship God? Why do people suffer? What is God's role in suffering?
2. The prologue in Job 1–2 shows us one approach to these questions (suffering as a test or growth opportunity). Other approaches are found in Job's speeches (we suffer because God is unjust); the friends' speeches (we've sinned and should turn away from sin, or God is trying to teach us something); God's speeches (suffering is a part of the real world where chaos and order are ever in tension); and the epilogue in Job 42 (there are rewards for faithfulness in the face of suffering).
3. A major question in Job and in other parts of scripture (such as Deuteronomy) is whether divine rewards and punishments make sense: Does good behavior bring happiness and blessing? Does bad behavior bring curse and suffering?
4. God's relationship with Job is at the heart of the story.

At the end of the viewing, choose one or two of the following questions to ask:

1. What kind of God do you see in the suffering of friends or even in your own life? Some answers include: God who punishes or rewards; God as unjust ruler; God as testing teacher who is leading you to a more mature faith; God as creator, balancing chaos and order; God as a present and compassionate friend.
2. Do you think people approach human suffering as an intellectual puzzle to be solved? A place to meet God? A place of divine absence?
3. What about suffering in your own life (or in the lives of those you know)? Tell stories with examples of both hard-won faith and soul-wrenching doubt in the face of suffering.

TAKE A BREAK (10 min. optional)

During the break, listen for participants' real feelings about this story that may or may not match their "on the record" comments in group discussion.

4. DISCOVERING TOGETHER (15 min.)

The last part of the story is in Job 42:7-17, as God awards Job with twice as many possessions as he lost. The Group Meeting Experience explores in detail the degree to which this is a satisfying conclusion to the story, or if it is a trite, awkward resolution to the complex questions that the book raises.

Divide the group into pairs, and invite each couple to work through the questions in the Group Meeting Experience portion of their participant guides together. Allow time for the group as a whole to share with each other their own conclusions about whether this ending to Job is satisfying or unsatisfying to them.

5. CENTERING TOGETHER (10 min. optional)

Job resonates at a deep level with our own suffering, and Job invites an empathy with those in our lives who are undergoing tragedy. We remember that despite its theological complexity, the story underscores this important lesson: Job didn't go through his suffering alone, and neither should any of us. Lead the group in an experience of Job 2:1-13, following the guidelines in the Covenant Meditation. Invite the group to share how this experience prompts them to share in the suffering of those they know.

6. SERVING TOGETHER (5 min.)

Read together the "Signs of Faithful Love" at the end of the episode. Break the participants into pairs, and have them review for a moment any notes they recorded and any insights they gained throughout this episode. Invite them to consider how the story of Job has revealed new insights into their own suffering, and how they will serve in practical ways to alleviate the suffering of others. You might lead the group in exploring a group mission project that assists those living in crisis.

7. NEXT WEEK (5 min.)

Turn to Episode 20 and briefly introduce next week's title and theme. Encourage participants to select a verse from the readings that they might commit to memory and share next week.

8. CLOSING PRAYER (5 min.)

Ask for any prayer concerns or joys, and invite participants to write these items down in the space provided under next week's Covenant Prayer. This way, the prayer needs will be in front of them as they read throughout the week. Close in a prayer together.

PARTICIPANT GUIDE 3

EPISODE 20—Jeremiah, Lamentations, Ezekiel

CRISIS AND STARTING OVER

When one covenant seems to end, start over again.

The fall of the northern kingdom to Assyria and the exile of the southern kingdom to Babylon were devastating events in Israel's history. Beyond the loss of land, the end of self-governance, and the destruction of the dearly loved temple, the crisis for the Israelites was theological in nature: Where was God in the midst of their suffering? What happened to God's covenant promise? Had it been revoked because of their sinful choices, or was there still the possibility of hope?

This week's readings sample three compelling responses to those questions, including:

Days 1–3: Jeremiah's emotional proclamations;
Day 4: Lamentation's witness of those who experienced the destruction firsthand; and
Day 5: Ezekiel's words among the exiled.

Today's episode will help your group:

- explore the difficult theological questions posed by the Israelite exile;
- discover how the prophets offered hope to devastated people; and
- incorporate that hope into their own experiences.

> **Materials needed:** *Covenant Leader Guide; Trusting the Covenant* participant guides; *CEB Study Bible; Trusting the Covenant* DVD (or video download); extra pens or pencils

1. GATHERING TOGETHER (10 min.)

Theological crises are a commonplace element of the Christian experience. There are moments when our perceptions of God and our expectations of how God will act do not adequately explain unfolding events. After praying the Covenant Prayer, invite the group to reflect together on moments when they experienced difficulties (for themselves, for people they know, or in the world at large) that defied their expectations of God. Or, as an alternative, hand out copies of hymns like "Great Is Thy Faithfulness" or "God Will Take Care of You." Invite participants to think of times when events were contrary to the promises contained in those hymns, and have them describe why those events are unsettling. Connect these feelings to those of the Israelite exiles in this week's readings.

> **Tip:** Do you trust God when things are falling apart? Acknowledge (and give the group permission to admit) that trusting God when things go wrong is very difficult. If some in the group find it easy to rush to trust (while others linger with their sorrow), help the group affirm and respect both postures.

2. REFLECTING TOGETHER (10 min.)

Read together "Our Longing for Relationship" at the beginning of Episode 20 in the participant guide. Invite participants to break up into pairs and share any passages from the week's readings that were particularly meaningful to them. Specifically, have group members explore the question: "What did these readings show you about God's attributes in the midst of suffering?" Have them share any insights they gained from the questions in the daily readings section of their participant guides. They might also share any verses they chose to memorize for the week.

Most of this week's readings come from Jeremiah, who makes it clear that the people's suffering is a direct result of their sinfulness and of the waywardness of their ancestors. Divide the participants into two groups, with one group examining the passages from Day 1 (Jer 1–4) and the other examining the passages from Day 3 (Jer 16; 18–20). Have them identify examples of how Jeremiah explains the people's suffering as a result of their sinfulness. What acts have they committed? After the groups share their discoveries, ask them to reflect together on the degree to which human suffering is a result of sinful choices. How do these passages reinforce the notion that sin has consequences?

Next, invite the group to reflect together on the reading from Day 2. Have someone read Jeremiah 27:12-15, and ask the group for their responses to the text. Jeremiah urges the people to accept their punishment. Can suffering ever be construed as productive punishment from God? What is either liberating or unsettling about this idea?

Finally, invite the participants to break back up into two groups, one to look at Lamentations 5 (from Day 4) and the other to look at Ezekiel 36–37 (from Day 5). Have the groups each make a list based on their readings: Group 1 will identify the words, phrases, and images that best describe moments when they have experienced grief, crisis, and despair. Group 2 will identify the words, phrases, and images that offer the most compelling hope to people in crisis. Have the groups share their lists, and invite them to make connections between suffering and hope. Is the hope contained in Ezekiel an adequate comfort to the anguish expressed in Lamentations? How is hope based not on evidence in the present, but on trust in God's faithfulness in the future?

3. VIDEO SEGMENT (25 min.)

The video for Episode 20, on the DVD or available by download, allows the group to overhear a conversation with Linda M. Day, who is a chaplain and Assistant Professor of Old Testament at Hiram College in Hiram, Ohio. Before showing the video, ask the participants to listen for one of the following key conversation points:

1. Jeremiah, Lamentations, and Ezekiel offer three different perspectives on the same catastrophe: the Babylonian destruction of Jerusalem and the kidnapping and captivity of God's people in a foreign land.

2. Lamentations is a "ground-zero" witness and liturgy of sorrow that speaks with little hope to the devastation of a people in the midst of disaster. Jeremiah blends God's sorrow with his own from a safer distance, while Ezekiel speaks from a visionary, priestly perspective far away in Babylon, dreaming vividly of a future glorious restoration of the temple.

3. These books affirm the power of lingering in the sorrow to hear the voices of those who are suffering through prayers of despair and confusion. These prayers connect the suffering ones to each other and to a shared hope that they will again trust God, who promises life for dry bones and a new covenant written on hearts in a blessed but distant future.

After viewing the video, choose one or two of the questions below to ask:

1. Do you remember where you were during a national crisis or tragedy (the assassination of a president, a terrorist attack, a natural disaster)? Recall the difference between early reports of what occurred and later, more distant analyses. How did people respond in the midst of the crisis? With despair and confusion? Anger and frustration? What about later?

2. Lamentations offers little in the way of hope, and yet it is a set of prayers unashamed to express grief and a shattered people's despair and confusion. What do you think about the idea that it is important to linger with sorrow for a time to give voice to the experience of suffering? Can rushing too quickly to words of hope silence the pain of those who need to be heard in their grief? Are you more of a "Let's linger in sorrow" type, or a silence the pain, "rush to hope" kind of person?

3. Think of "dry bones" in the desert of your own life (delayed or broken dreams, distant or present grief, losses or setbacks that seem insurmountable). Does it seem possible (or impossible) that these "dry bones" might live again? What role does imagining or having a vision for a restored future play in your own faith and prayer life?

TAKE A BREAK (10 min. optional)

Exile is disaster. Listen during the break for participants' laughter or other coping mechanisms for dealing with disaster.

4. DISCOVERING TOGETHER (15 min.)

Even with its painful assessment of despair and crisis, the book of Jeremiah concludes with a grand, compelling promise of restoration. The Group Meeting Experience investigates the beautiful words of Jeremiah 31:15-34, in which God promises to engrave a new covenant on the hearts of the people. Break the participants into four or five groups and have each group answer one of the five questions in the exercise. Have them all share their conclusions with each other.

5. CENTERING TOGETHER (10 min. optional)

Personal crisis is just as threatening as a crisis faced by an entire community. For example, in several passionate confessions Jeremiah expressed deep anguish over his mission from the Lord.

Have the group break up into pairs and follow the instructions for the Covenant Meditation based on Lamentations 3:1-24 in their participant guides. Through the exercise, invite each participant to share with their partner the situation that is prompting this desperate plea for help. When the group comes back together, ask them what barriers might prevent them from praying in this way and how those barriers can be overcome.

6. SERVING TOGETHER (5 min.)

Read together the "Signs of Faithful Love" at the end of the episode. Break the participants into pairs, and have them review for a moment any notes they recorded and any insights they gained throughout this episode. Invite group members to share how these insights will encourage them to have hope in the midst of despair and to become a source of hope for specific people in crisis.

7. NEXT WEEK (5 min.)

Turn to Episode 21 and briefly introduce next week's title and theme. Encourage participants to select a verse from the readings that they might commit to memory and share next week.

8. CLOSING PRAYER (5 min.)

Ask for any prayer concerns or joys, and invite participants to write these items down in the space provided under next week's Covenant Prayer. This way, the prayer needs will be in front of them as they read throughout the week. Close in a prayer together.

PARTICIPANT GUIDE 3
EPISODE 21—Isaiah 40-66
EXILE AND RENEWAL
The risk of being in charge

Some participants may have doubts about dividing Isaiah into three documents. If so, allow a moment for the group to question the evidence for the three sections; but of course, focus on the message for a people in exile rather than the editorial history of the prophetic book. Isaiah 40–66 has two concurrent messages for the exiles. First, there is good news: God will be faithful to lead them home. God is revealed as:

Day 1: their powerful creator;
Day 2: their comforter;
Day 3: their restorer;
Day 4: the one who seeks justice; and
Day 5: the one who will always be with them.

However, their experience of home will be unlike their lives in the past. The exiles will have to expand their theology, their sense of mission, and their understanding of covenant to adapt to a changed world.

This episode will help your group:

- recognize the main divine characteristics of God described in Isaiah 40–66;
- learn how the Israelites had to adapt to their new surroundings; and
- investigate how these adaptations translate to the nature and mission of the church today.

> **Materials needed:** *Covenant Leader Guide*; *Trusting the Covenant* participant guides; *CEB Study Bible*; *Trusting the Covenant* DVD (or video download); extra pens or pencils

1. GATHERING TOGETHER (10 min.)

After the Covenant Prayer, invite participants to reflect on what the word *home* means to them. Ask if there has ever been a time when they returned home after a very long time of being away. What was the same? What was different? How had they changed in the interim?

2. REFLECTING TOGETHER (10 min.)

Read together "Our Longing for Relationship" at the beginning of the episode. Invite participants to break up into pairs and share any passages from the week's readings that were particularly meaningful to them. Isaiah 40–66 contains passages that are quoted the most in other parts of the scriptures. Ask if the participants recognize any other places in the Bible that quote Isaiah and which verses are particularly meaningful to them. (The *CEB Study Bible* has cross-references.) Have them share any insights they gained from the questions in the daily readings section of their participant guides. They might also share any verses they chose to memorize for the week.

Divide the group into five subgroups, and have each group explore a different characteristic of God's faithfulness that is demonstrated in the daily readings:

1. God as creator (Isa 40:12-25; 42:5-9);
2. God as comforter (Isa 40:1-5; 51:1-6, 12-16);
3. God as restorer (Isa 43:1-13; 55:1-13);
4. God who assures justice (Isa 58:1-14); and
5. God's dwelling with us (Isa 65:17-25; 66:1-2).

Invite the individual subgroups to answer these questions for each category above: "What words or phrases in these passages describe God in this way? How might this characteristic of God have been good news to people in exile?"

Though the people gradually returned home, they realized that life was going to be much different for them from in the past. Divide the participants into four groups, and invite each group to explore a change in the theology and mission of the Israelites that was a result of the exile:

1. God is universal, rather than merely the God of Israel (Isa 40:12-25);
2. God's covenant is with all Israelites, not just with the celebrated heroes of the faith (Isa 41:8-20);
3. "God's servant" is the Persian king Cyrus, rather than an Israelite king in the line of David (Isa 41:1-4; 42:1-4; 45:1-8); and
4. the mission of the Israelites is to extend social justice to the outcasts (Isa 56:1-8).

For each category, ask these questions: "How do you think this new understanding was shaped by the events of the exile? How much of a difference do you think this made in the way the Israelites perceived God, themselves, and their purpose as the people of God?" Invite the groups to report their conclusions to the rest of the participants.

> **Tip:** Imagine that each person in your group will soon encounter God in the ways described in Reflecting Together. See them as recipients and conduits of God's grace in this Covenant group and in the broader community.

3. VIDEO SEGMENT (25 min.)

The video for Episode 21, on the DVD or available by download, allows the group to overhear a conversation with Patricia K. Tull, who is a retired Professor of Old Testament at Louisville Presbyterian Theological Seminary. Before showing the video, ask the participants to listen for one or more of the following key conversation points:

1. The story of how Israel gained and lost the land becomes the treasured object the people carry with them into exile. This is never boiled down to a single story but remains a larger, ongoing conversation that will shape their hearts and lives as they long for home in exile.

2. Isaiah 40–55 (Second Isaiah) and Isaiah 56–66 (Third Isaiah) continue the powerful poetry found in First Isaiah of Jerusalem (Isa 1–39). They are written to inspire and invite God's homesick (but also complacent) people in Babylon to become pioneers—when returning home seems neither possible nor even the natural next step for their community.

3. The conventional wisdom of the time held that a god was tied to the boundaries of a given region and landscape. Against this common idea, the prophet declares that the God of Israel is God everywhere, all the time. The people might have left God's country, but God has not left them. Instead, the God of Israel is the best and only God, traveling with and caring for the people even in a distant land. Ever-present through the fire and chaos of captivity, God says, "Don't fear, for I have redeemed you; I have called you by name; you are mine" (Isa 43:1b).

After viewing the video, choose one or two of these questions to ask:

1. If your house were on fire or you were being evacuated from your home and couldn't return, what one or two things would you grab or take with you (after family members and pets, of course)? Why would you choose these items? Would other family members in your house grab something else? What do these objects symbolize, or what memories do they gather for you? Do you know anyone who lost everything in a fire or disaster? What if all you had left was your story?

2. Why do you think it would be a "pioneering" decision for the people of Israel to return home from Babylon? Another writer (Tom Wolfe) once said you can't go home again. Isaiah says you can, you will, and God will go with you. Which view comes closest to your own experiences with homecoming? Is it possible that exile is easier and more familiar than going "home" to a place you've never seen?

3. It's hard to relate to a culture that thought divine powers were tied to local landscapes. Have you ever felt that "you weren't in Kansas anymore" or that the house rules and practices of where you come from didn't work in a new place?

TAKE A BREAK (10 min. optional)

Find a way to help one person feel that they have a home in this group.

4. DISCOVERING TOGETHER (15 min.)

The experience of exile necessarily broadened the theology of the Israelites to perceive God as the creator of the cosmos, rather than as a provincial God of the promised land. The Group Meeting Experience is an effective way to compare and contrast the creation narrative of Genesis with the theology about the divine creator in Isaiah. Invite the participants to divide into groups of three and work through the questions in the exercise, and have them share their findings with the rest of the participants.

5. CENTERING TOGETHER (10 min. optional)

Isaiah 40–66 contains profound words of hope and comfort for people experiencing their own kind of exile. The Covenant Meditation in this episode can be deeply helpful for people undergoing personal crises, so allow time to lead group members through the exercise and to process it afterward. Invite people to share with the group how the words of Isaiah 43:1-7 are helpful to them now.

6. SERVING TOGETHER (5 min.)

Read together the "Signs of Faithful Love" at the end of the episode. Break the participants into pairs, and have them review for a moment any notes they recorded and any insights they gained throughout this episode. Invite them to consider how the oracles of Isaiah can translate into tangible actions that they can take this week to receive the good news of God, to broaden their theology, and to bring hope and comfort to others in exile.

7. NEXT WEEK (5 min.)

Turn to Episode 22 and briefly introduce next week's title and theme. Encourage participants to select a verse from the readings that they might commit to memory and share next week. Be sure to mention that there are additional videos available at CovenantBibleStudy.com for participants who want to enhance their study throughout the week.

8. CLOSING PRAYER (5 min.)

Ask for any prayer concerns or joys, and invite participants to write these items down in the space provided under next week's Covenant Prayer. This way, the prayer needs will be in front of them as they read throughout the week. Close in a prayer together.

PARTICIPANT GUIDE 3

EPISODE 22—1 and 2 Chronicles, Ezra, Nehemiah

RESTORATION

Rebuilding life together

When Persia's King Cyrus granted the Israelites their return from exile, they had one primary purpose in mind: renew their worship of God. To do that, they needed to reinstitute three key ingredients, all of which are covered in this week's readings:

Day 3: they needed a place to worship, which was rebuilt under Zerubbabel and others;
Day 4: they needed a people whose hearts and behaviors were right with God; and
Day 5: they needed a heart of praise, which came after Nehemiah rebuilt the walls of Jerusalem.

This episode will help your group:

- learn the time line of key events involved in the exiles' return to Jerusalem;
- investigate the key elements of place, people, and praise instituted by Zerubbabel, Ezra, and Nehemiah, which were all crucial in returning people to righteous worship; and
- explore how these ingredients can inform a renewal of worship in the participants' own congregation.

Materials needed: *Covenant Leader Guide*; *Trusting the Covenant* participant guides; *CEB Study Bible*; *Trusting the Covenant* DVD (or video download); extra pens or pencils; blank paper

Optional: An additional video on exile and the return to worship in Jerusalem is available for download from CovenantBibleStudy.com.

1. GATHERING TOGETHER (10 min.)

Read the Covenant Prayer together. Invite group members to reflect on a time when they experienced a significant rebuilding project on a home, a church, or some other place of significance. What obstacles did they overcome? More importantly, what kind of inner strength did they have to develop, and how were they changed in the process?

2. REFLECTING TOGETHER (10 min.)

Read together "Our Longing for Relationship" at the beginning of the episode. To gain a full appreciation of the material covered in these books, establish a clear time line of the major events involved in the exiles' return. (It may also be helpful to consult the *CEB Bible Map Guide* to get a better idea of where the exiles' journey took them.) Divide the group into smaller groups, and assign them the following scriptures to look up, in the noted chronological order. Have them determine the major event that is described in each passage (which is provided here in parentheses next to each reference), along with the approximate year the event occurred. Together, construct a time line of events that can serve as the backbone for the rest of this episode's discussions.

1. Ezra 1:2-4; 6:3-5 (edict of King Cyrus, 539 BCE)
2. Ezra 1:5; 2 (first wave of exiles returns)
3. Ezra 3:1-13 (work on temple begins, 535 BCE)
4. Ezra 4:24 (Darius becomes king of Persia, 522 BCE)
5. Ezra 5:1-2 (temple is completed under Zerubbabel, 516 BCE)
6. Esther 1:1 (Ahasuerus becomes king of Persia, 485 BCE)
7. Ezra 7:12-13 (Artaxerxes becomes king of Persia, 465 BCE)
8. Ezra 9–10 (religious reform of the people under Ezra, 458 BCE)
9. Nehemiah 1–2 (another wave of exiles returns under Nehemiah to rebuild the wall, 433 BCE)

With the time line constructed, divide the participants into three groups, and have them reflect on the readings from Days 3–5. Have the group working on Day 3 discuss why the rebuilding of the altar and the temple was important for renewing worship. Have the group working on Day 4 discuss the nature of the religious reforms instituted by Ezra and why they were critical in renewing worship. Have the group working on Day 5 focus particularly on Nehemiah 8:9-18 and the command to rejoice and have hearts of praise. How is this command an important ingredient in the renewal of worship?

When all the groups have reported their conclusions, invite the participants to reflect together on how their congregations can experience a renewal of worship following the examples prescribed in these texts.

> **Tip:** It takes time to rebuild a life after years of homeless exile. Ask God to give you and your group patience for the rebuilding project going on in the lives of loved ones and of each other.

3. VIDEO SEGMENT (25 min.)

The video for Episode 22, on the DVD or available by download, allows the group to overhear a conversation with Melody D. Knowles, who is Associate Professor of Old Testament at Virginia Theological Seminary in Alexandria, Virginia. Before showing the video, ask the participants to listen for one or more of the following conversation points:

1. The people returning home from exile in successive waves must rebuild a whole new way of life from almost nothing. Ezra and Nehemiah look at the present and at the practical need for rebuilding city walls and a center for worship. The Chronicler emphasizes that the people would need to interpret their story correctly and remember who they were from the beginning if they were going to move forward and make a new life out of the rubble.

2. For the returnees, the work of identity is a difficult process. It involves defining the community and answering the question "Who are we?" in the midst of a mess. The returnees agree on certain things (worship of God in Jerusalem) but wrestle with others (intermarriage with those outside the community). Ezra and Nehemiah see this as a problem to be remedied by exiling foreign wives, while the Chronicler sees this practice as one that can strengthen the community (recall this view in the book of Ruth). But all understand that the stakes are high if they get it wrong: A broken covenant with God meant exile for their grandparents' generation.

3. The practices that sustained the people in exile (circumcision, Sabbath keeping, and so on) continue to define a people who are not from the same generation that left Israel in chains fifty or more years before. Even those left behind in Israel during the exile will struggle as they restart and reboot their lives.

After viewing the video, ask one or two of these questions:

1. Ask the participants to think of a time when they had to begin again or start over from scratch. Was it hard to know where to start? Why do the returning exiles begin with the temple and the city walls? How can a "back to the basics" or "focus on the fundamentals" approach help you begin again?

2. The Chronicler believes it is crucial that the people retell their story when starting over. Think of someone in your life who began again by retelling their story from a "starting-over" perspective. Have you retold your story in light of a new beginning?

3. Make a list of things you need when making a fresh start (the essentials) and the things better left behind (the clutter). What makes it hard to restart or reboot our own lives? Recall the practices from our study of the prophets that sent the people into exile (worshipping other gods, injustice and mistreating the vulnerable, trusting accomplishment rather than God).

TAKE A BREAK (10 min. optional)

Tell someone in the group who lives alone (or who seems lonely) that you value their participation.

4. DISCOVERING TOGETHER (15 min.)

The Group Meeting Experience refocuses the episode on the central idea of this study: the covenant relationship between God and God's people. David's final prayer in 1 Chronicles 29:10-19 is a rich resource for remembering who God is, who we are, and who we are called to be as a covenant people. Invite the group to work in pairs through the questions in the exercise, and have them share their conclusions with the group.

5. CENTERING TOGETHER (10 min. optional)

The text offered in this week's Covenant Meditation, 2 Chronicles 15:12-15, embodies the ideal characteristics of a covenant people rightly oriented toward God. Lead the group in the exercise, or allow time for those who did the exercise on their own to share some aspects of their experiences with the group.

6. SERVING TOGETHER (5 min.)

Read together the "Signs of Faithful Love" at the end of the episode. Break the participants into pairs, and have them review for a moment any notes they recorded and any insights they gained throughout this episode. Invite them to consider how these texts will shape their behavior this week, and have them share with a partner some practical ways they will pursue worship-renewal in their hearts and in their churches.

7. NEXT WEEK (5 min.)

Turn to Episode 23 and briefly introduce next week's title and theme. Encourage participants to select a verse from the readings that they might commit to memory and share next week. Be sure to mention that there are additional videos available at CovenantBibleStudy.com for participants who want to enhance their study throughout the week.

8. CLOSING PRAYER (5 min.)

Ask for any prayer concerns or joys, and invite participants to write these items down in the space provided under next week's Covenant Prayer. This way, the prayer needs will be in front of them as they read throughout the week. Close in a prayer together.

PARTICIPANT GUIDE 3
EPISODE 23—Apocalyptic: Daniel
HOPE
Trusting God in times of crisis

Reading an apocalyptic book or passage is a mystifying experience. The texts are easily misunderstood and misapplied, especially if the reader, hundreds of years later, speculates about the symbols, plotlines, and characters. What do we do with all the fanciful imagery and bizarre symbols? Your group's work with the book of Daniel will spark creative imagination and elicit a diversity of opinions regarding this important period of Jewish experience (and Christian experience, when discussing Revelation in Episode 24). In particular, this episode will engage your group in relevant questions regarding the relationship between the church and the state, between our participation in God's kingdom while living among the empires on earth.

This episode will help your group:

* become familiar with the story of Daniel in its imagined and actual historical context;
* use the narrative to engage in a discussion about political empires and God's kingdom; and
* discover how Daniel's prayer might serve as a model of confession for us now.

Materials needed: *Covenant Leader Guide*; *Trusting the Covenant* participant guides; *CEB Study Bible*; *Trusting the Covenant* DVD (or video download); extra pens or pencils; photocopies of the "More Signs of Faithful Love" handout to pass out at the end of the meeting; poster board or butcher paper; markers or crayons for drawing

Optional: An additional video on how contemporary communities identify with stories about Daniel is available for download from CovenantBibleStudy.com. There is also a video on the "one like a human being" (or "Son of Man") and Jesus, as well as a video retelling the story of Shadrach, Meshach, and Abednego.

1. GATHERING TOGETHER (10 min.)

After reading the Covenant Prayer, ask participants to reflect together on the importance of dreams. Expand the discussion to include dreams during slumber and dreams related to imagination, visioning, and goal setting. Why are dreams important to have? What significance do you give to dreams you have while you sleep? What role do "dreamers" play in our churches and in our culture?

2. REFLECTING TOGETHER (10 min.)

Read together "Our Longing for Relationship" at the beginning of Episode 23 in the participant guide. Invite participants to break up into pairs and share any passages from the week's readings that were particularly meaningful. Have them share any insights they gained about Daniel from the questions in the daily readings section of their participant guides. They might also share any verses they chose to memorize for the week.

The most important dream in the book of Daniel is offered by King Nebuchadnezzar in a portion of the reading for Day 1: Daniel 2:31-35. Have the group work together to draw a picture of the statue from the dream, and invite them to label the body parts with the corresponding historical empires. Remind the group that the book of Daniel was written retrospectively, during a time of intense oppression during the Seleucid period, as outlined in the participant guide.

The readings in the first three days invite reflections on the relationship between the faith community and political kingdoms. Divide the group into three smaller subgroups, and ask them to explore:

1. the temporal nature of the kingdoms of the earth (Day 1: Political empires will eventually fade, but God's kingdom is eternal);
2. the dual nature of the earth's empires (Day 2: Political kingdoms have the capacity to improve people's lives or to cause great harm); and
3. the nature of civil disobedience (Day 3: The story promotes effective, nonviolent forms of protest).

For each category, invite the group to answer the question: "What do these readings suggest to you about the relationship between the present-day church and the state?"

3. VIDEO SEGMENT (25 min.)

The video for Episode 23, on the DVD or available by download, gives the group a chance to overhear a conversation with Daniel L. Smith-Christopher, who is Professor of Theological Studies and Director of Peace Studies at Loyola Marymount College in Los Angeles, California. Before showing the video, ask the participants to listen for one or more of the following conversation points:

1. Apocalyptic (meaning "to be revealed") literature is not primarily about future events. People tend to see these books as future texts because the stories seem relevant to our situation, giving

us a sense that in times of crisis there is a divine plan at work. During a global crisis, or even an anniversary of a crisis (such as in the year 2000), speculation about apocalyptic literature grows through attempts to decode ancient symbols and vivid images. It's okay to go to this literature for a sense of reassurance that God is ultimately sovereign.

2. Daniel was probably written during the brutal reign of the Greek (Seleucid) ruler Antiochus Epiphanes IV (167–164 BCE). The court stories of Daniel press us to think about and measure the cost of discipleship. Faith has its price. The book of Daniel is about the covenant people's struggle for identity and the challenge of living in a context where faithfulness is under threat.

3. People living under the impact of a dominant culture read Daniel with a better grasp of what's at stake when you're trying to hold on to who you are. Yet this literature is about hope. It says, "Don't give up—because ultimately, God is in control."

After viewing the video, ask one or two of the following questions:

1. Can you think of examples of books or movies that use apocalyptic literature to speculate about the future? Why do you think some people want to know the future? How is our twenty-first-century speculation about the end of the world different from or similar to what was going on when the book of Daniel was written?

2. It's been said that if you eat at the king's table, you become the king's woman or man. What forces demand our loyalty today? How do our culture and other forces work to erase our covenant identity? If God's love is ultimately in control, how might that change our relationship to these other powers? Can we say with Shadrach (Hananiah), Meshach (Mishael), and Abednego (Azariah): "If [God] doesn't [rescue us] . . . we will never serve your gods or worship the gold statue you've set up" (Dan 3:18)?

3. Do you find hope in the Daniel stories? How do stories of stubborn hope help us wait together for God's love and power to show up? If hope is a courage and confidence that God's goodness will win the day, what are some contemporary stories of courageous hope?

TAKE A BREAK (10 min. optional)

During the break, praise or celebrate someone in your group out loud.

4. DISCOVERING TOGETHER (15 min.)

The Group Meeting Experience invites a closer look at the relationship between divine and political powers using Daniel 11:27-35. Divide the participants into smaller groups and ask each subgroup to reflect on one of the five questions in the exercise. Leave time for groups to report their conclusions to the whole group.

5. CENTERING TOGETHER (10 min. optional)

The narratives in Daniel are full of inspiring stories of courage in the midst of adversity, claiming hope in the midst of chaos. The Covenant Meditation on Daniel 9:4-19 provides an excellent way to fortify one's personal life with the words of scripture. With such courage and hope, we can face any difficulties in life. Lead the group in the meditation, and leave time for participants to share their insights.

6. SERVING TOGETHER (5 min.)

Read together the "Signs of Faithful Love" at the end of the episode. Break the participants into pairs, and have them review for a moment any notes they recorded and any insights they gained throughout this episode. Invite them to consider how these texts will shape their behavior this week, and have them share with a partner one practical way they will live out the lessons from this episode.

7. NEXT WEEK (5 min.)

Turn to Episode 24 and briefly introduce the final week's title and theme. Encourage participants to select a verse from the readings that they might commit to memory and share next week.

Next week the group will conclude Covenant Bible Study with a shared meal. Have the group make plans for the meal and for what each person should bring. Also make copies of the "More Signs of Faithful Love" handout at the back of this leader guide and pass them out. Encourage participants to go to CovenantBibleStudy.com before the next meeting and click on the link for Spiritual Gifts and Growth Tools. At that link, they will find two types of personal inventories that can help them identify and share more signs of faithful love: a spiritual gifts assessment tool and a spiritual growth assessment tool. Instruct the group members to use these tools sometime during the next week and to bring their results to share with the rest of the group next week. This final meeting will last two hours.

8. CLOSING PRAYER (5 min.)

Ask for any prayer concerns or joys, and invite participants to write these items down in the space provided under next week's Covenant Prayer. This way, the prayer needs will be in front of them as they read throughout the week. Close in a prayer together.

PARTICIPANT GUIDE 3

EPISODE 24—Revelation

NEW CREATION

Trusting God, who makes all things new

PREPARATION BEFORE EPISODE 24:

- Allow two hours for this final group meeting experience and meal.
- Make arrangements for a celebratory meal to be shared by the group participants.
- Queue up and preview the two videos for this episode.
- Make copies of (or project on a screen) the response "Our Covenant." (A reproducible handout is found at the back of this leader guide.)
- Have extra copies of the "More Signs of Faithful Love" handout (also available at the back of this leader guide) for any participants who didn't use the spiritual gifts and spiritual growth assessment tools before the meeting.

Our journey concludes with one more event. This final episode culminates the sweeping movement of God's love through every book of the Bible by exploring the spiritual exodus led by Christ to the New Jerusalem. Each of the week's readings reveals the rich, mysterious imagery of Revelation. This final episode in human history invites the reader to connect with its overarching themes of courage, perseverance, and hope. The final group meeting contains a review of the Covenant Bible Study experience, including a recommitment to participating in God's renewal of the world. It concludes with the sharing of a meal.

This episode will help your group:

- connect the original context of Revelation to the issues facing the church today;
- discover ways to apply the message of Revelation for today; and
- recommit their lives to God's work in the world.

Materials needed: *Covenant Leader Guide*; *Trusting the Covenant* participant guides; *CEB Study Bible*; *Trusting the Covenant* DVD (or video download); extra pens or pencils; photocopies of the "Our Covenant" and "More Signs of Faithful Love" double-sided handout; supplies for a shared meal; a digital camera for a group picture; a thoughtful list of qualities you have witnessed in each person in the group during this journey together

....

Optional: Compare the participants' qualities to qualities found in covenant people in scripture. Also, please note that two video clips will be played for this final episode. One features Revelation and the other brief clip is a closing message from the hosts.

1. GATHERING TOGETHER (10 min.)

Read the Covenant Prayer together, and invite the group to reflect on their preconceived notions of the book of Revelation. What impressions did they have about the book prior to this week's study? Invite participants to reflect on ways that popular culture (books, movies, songs, art) has shaped the way they considered the book in the past. What has troubled them about the book? What do they hope to discover in this meeting?

2. REFLECTING TOGETHER (10 min.)

Read together "Our Longing for Relationship" at the beginning of the episode. Invite participants to break up into pairs and share any passages from the week's readings that were particularly meaningful. Have them share any insights they gained from the questions in the daily readings section of their participant guides. Remind them that the original audience for Revelation was a regional community experiencing severe harassment by the Roman Empire. What particular passages from the week's readings would have offered comfort to a community under distress? What comfort might they bring to the church today? Participants might also share any verses they chose to memorize for the week.

Divide the group into pairs or into small subgroups, and invite group members to cover each of the seven churches described in the readings for Day 1. Have them decide how God's assessment of that particular church is similar to their local congregations or to the wider church today. What praiseworthy qualities are similar? What weaknesses do they share?

Each of the remaining daily readings offers a different dimension to the common theme of Revelation: "Faithfulness will be costly, but it will be rewarded in the end." Display that statement for the group, and break them up into four new subgroups to explore each of the remaining daily readings. What elements of each reading reinforce that central theme? What does this reading suggest is the cost of faithful living? What is the promised reward?

3. VIDEO SEGMENT (15 min.)

The video for Episode 24, on the DVD or available by download, allows the group to overhear a conversation with Thomas B. Slater, who is Professor of New Testament Language and Literature at McAfee School of Theology in Atlanta, Georgia. Before showing the video, ask the participants to listen for one or more of the following conversation points:

1. Revelation is a book written for people who were poor and struggling under great duress. It uses vivid, sometimes terrifying images to express the centrality of God's unswerving faithfulness and the faithfulness of those who stand firm in the face of dehumanizing forces in the world.

2. Like the faithfulness of the Lamb and of the saints who overcome evil through their willingness to die for what is right, the faithfulness depicted in the book of Revelation is grounded by hope in God, who will save and set things right.

3. The symbol of hope in Revelation is the new creation and covenant of love between God and the faithful. This symbol of new creation provides comfort, courage, and the assurance that the one who made a covenant with all things at the very beginning will be with us at the end of all things. The Holy Spirit is the present foretaste of this new creation, giving us life in the here and now.

After viewing the first video on Revelation (time permitting), ask the group one of the following questions:

1. Have you or someone you know ever read this book in the way one reads tea leaves to decipher details about the "last days"? How has this book been used in popular fiction to portray the "end time"? Is this missing the point (God's faithfulness and new creation)? Why does Revelation frighten so many people? Does it frighten you? Why would people living under oppression find this picture of God's faithfulness so compelling? What does it mean to stand firm and listen to the Holy Spirit among the empires of today's world?

2. Is the new creation described in Revelation 21 a symbol of hope to you? How does it echo, or form a "bookend," for the covenants in Genesis with Abraham and Noah and the Exodus covenant at Sinai? Can you imagine a world where disease and suffering don't get the last word? How can this hope stir us to create, here and now, a taste of that coming new creation (vanquished disease, eased pain, tears wiped away)?

4. DISCOVERING TOGETHER (15 min.)

The Group Meeting Experience explores the resolution that Revelation provides to the creation story introduced in Genesis. Invite the group to work together to compile two lists. The first should be headed with the statement "The story of the Bible begins with . . . ," and the group can fill it in with problems and crises introduced in the Genesis creation stories. The second should be headed with the statement "And the story of the Bible ends with . . . ," and the group can fill it in with the corresponding ways that Revelation may or may not bring resolution to the Genesis creation narrative.

5. CENTERING TOGETHER (10 min. optional)

Remind the group that the book of Revelation is a "noisy" book, intended to be experienced audibly and visually. The Covenant Meditation in this episode creates an immersive encounter with Revelation 7:9-17. Lead them through the exercise, and process it afterward.

6. CLOSING VIDEO SEGMENT (5 min.)

Play the three-minute wrap-up video featuring concluding comments from the hosts. The wrap-up video offers an invitation for participants to continue the discipline of personal Bible study, to determine their spiritual gifts, and to find ways to serve God in and through the church.

After you play the wrap-up video, distribute copies of the double-sided handout found at the end of this leader guide. The "More Signs of Faithful Love" side includes instructions for going online to take two personal questionnaires that will help participants discern what's next for their spiritual growth. The first online survey (available at CovenantBibleStudy.com) helps a person figure out their spiritual gifts and the corresponding places of service that are vital in any congregation. The other survey helps a participant identify ways to grow more deeply as a spiritual being.

For any participants who completed these personal inventories in the past week, use this time to let them share their results. Encourage them to give specific examples of how they will serve and grow.

7. CELEBRATION AND RENEWAL (5 min.)

Gather the participants for a meal. Distribute the double-sided reproducible handout (found at the end of this leader guide) to the participants if you didn't already do so after the wrap-up video. The "Our Covenant" liturgy serves as a recap of the major highlights from the Covenant Bible Study experience. With everyone seated at the table, lead the group in the responsive "Our Covenant" service.

8. SHARING OF THE MEAL (30 min.)

As participants partake of the meal, invite people to share:

- qualities they have witnessed in each person in the group (and how these are like specific covenant people from scripture);
- a significant learning they received from this study;
- one area of life that has been significantly affected by this study; and
- a way they will express what they've learned through tangible service in the church and the community.

Close in a prayer together, and stay in touch, caring for each other. Challenge each participant to become involved in a ministry at their church.

OUR COVENANT

LEADER: God of power and love, through whom all things were created, and in whom all things are being re-created, we give you thanks for this meal and for gathering us around this table. We rejoice in your presence in the midst of our lives, guiding us along a journey of fellowship, renewal, and discovery of your Word for us.

PARTICIPANTS: Anoint us with your Spirit in the sharing of this meal.

LEADER: We give thanks for the unique relationship with you that you have given to us. We acknowledge this relationship throughout the scriptures, beginning with the call you gave humans at the moment of creation to care for the earth and to participate in its beauty and sustenance.

PARTICIPANTS: In this covenant we commit ourselves to care for the earth.

LEADER: We remember the promise you made with Abraham and Sarah, rewarding their faithfulness with a special promise about who would carry forth your faithful love. We give you thanks that we are part of that inheritance, a visible fulfillment of your promise.

PARTICIPANTS: In this covenant we commit ourselves to faithfully follow what you promised to future generations.

LEADER: We remember the promise you made to Moses and to the liberated Israelites, leading them through the wilderness and ordering their lives with instructions that would preserve their relationships, honor all life, and bring praise to you.

PARTICIPANTS: In this covenant we commit ourselves to holy living and to doing the right thing in every circumstance.

LEADER: We remember the promise you made with David, that in your goodness your participants would receive the provision of land, a glorious place to worship, and the security of leadership.

PARTICIPANTS: In this covenant we commit ourselves to obey your ways.

LEADER: We give you thanks for the gift of Jesus, who suffered, died, and rose again to begin a new covenant based on forgiveness and grace. We give thanks for your Holy Spirit, who gives birth to the church, the body of Christ, which spreads God's faithful love throughout the world.

PARTICIPANTS: In this covenant, with the help and comfort of the Holy Spirit, we commit ourselves to faithful love, which has no greater example than the faithfulness of Jesus on the cross.

LEADER: *(With all joining hands around the table)* Gracious God, as we share this meal now, we renew our commitment to serve you in the world. We thank you for your abundance, while we remember those who are hungry today. We thank you for your faithful love, while we remember to find those who feel unloved. We thank you for your hope, while we remember those who live in despair.

PARTICIPANTS: *(Still with hands joined)* Pour out your Holy Spirit upon us. Make us one with Christ, and one in service to the world. In the name of Jesus Christ we pray, amen.

(ALL RECITE THE LORD'S PRAYER)

(ALL SHARE SIGNS OF PEACE AND RECONCILIATION WITH EACH OTHER)

MORE SIGNS OF FAITHFUL LOVE

Covenant Bible Study is a rewarding challenge for any Christian learner. And you met the challenge! You made friends for life, and the Bible became an even deeper friend for life.

So what's next for your spiritual journey? Covenant Bible Study offers two types of personal inventories that can help you identify and share more signs of faithful love in your church and in your personal walk with God.

Go to CovenantBibleStudy.com. Click on the link for Spiritual Gifts and Growth Tools.

One inventory is a spiritual gifts assessment tool. It contains eighty-five questions. Every one of us has spiritual gifts that are vital to the body of Christ. This spiritual gifts tool will help you figure out what part of Christ's body needs you the most.

The second spiritual growth assessment tool contains forty questions about your (personal) beliefs about the world, relationships, yourself, and work. Your score on this survey will result in a set of immediate suggestions for further spiritual development.